NORTHERN APPALACHIA REVIEW

VOLUME 3

CATAMOUNT
PRESS

an imprint of Sunbury Press, Inc.
Mechanicsburg, PA USA

CATAMOUNT
PRESS

an imprint of Sunbury Press, Inc.
Mechanicsburg, PA USA

For information about special discounts for bulk purchases, please contact Sunbury Press Orders Dept. at (855) 338-8359 or orders@sunburypress.com.

To request one of our authors for speaking engagements or book signings, please contact Sunbury Press Publicity Dept. at publicity@sunburypress.com.

FIRST CATAMOUNT PRESS EDITION: March 2022

Set in Adobe Garamond.

Publisher's Cataloging-in-Publication Data
Names: PJ Piccirillo, et al.
Title: Northern Appalachia Review Volume 3.
Description: First trade paperback edition. | Mechanicsburg, PA : Catamount Press, 2022.
Summary: An academic literary journal focused on writers from the northern Appalachia region.
Identifiers: ISBN: 978-1-62006-913-4 (softcover).
Subjects: FICTION / Anthologies | LITERARY COLLECTIONS / American / General | FICTION / Cultural Heritage.

Product of the United States of America
0 1 1 2 3 5 8 13 21 34 55

Continue the Enlightenment!

Northern Appalachia Review

Editor-in-Chief and Founding Editor:
PJ Piccirillo

Nonfiction Editor: Carrie Hohmann Campbell
Fiction Editor: Virginia Rafferty
Poetry Editor: William Scott Hanna
Editor, Book Reviews, Interviews, and Literature of the Outdoors and Environment: Dominique Hoche
Copy Editor: Rita Wilson
Managing Editor: Samantha Backstrom
Assistant Poetry Editor: Kathleen S. Burgess
Assistant Copy Editor: Debra Reynolds

Fiction Readers
Samantha Backstrom
Nicole Ravas
Debra Reynolds
Arthur Turfa

Poetry Readers
Carrie Hohmann Campbell
Matthew Vargo

Nonfiction Readers
Rita Wilson
Debra Reynolds

Administrative Coordinator:
Nicole Ravas

Production Coordinator:
Debra Reynolds

Cover Photo: David A. Woodring
Cover Art: Leonard Treat
Cover Designer: Lawrence Knorr
Book Designer: Crystal Devine

Advisory Board
Brad Barkley
Bonnie Culver
Marc Harshman
Gerry LaFemina
Nancy McKinley
David Poyer

The Northern Appalachia Review publishes once annually. U.S. subscription rate is $15 for one copy. See submissions guidelines at NorthernAppReview.com. Address all correspondence to The Editors, generalinquiries@NorthernAppReview.com.

CONTENTS

INTRODUCTION

The work of Leonard Treat (1926-2006), which graces the cover of this volume, is a visual counterpart to much of the literature of northern Appalachia. Leonard's work remains obscure and underappreciated. But those who've seen the figures he carved—"whittled," he liked to say—know they're brilliant. The personalities of his pieces are as rich and distinct as the grain of the basswood he preferred for his carvings. Leonard's hand had something akin to what writers strive for: voice—that one-in-a-million fingerprint.

Aside from his time on the USS Torrance during World War II, Leonard spent his life in Pennsylvania's Potter County, in the heart of northern Appalachia. Known throughout the commonwealth as "God's Country," the county is rich in lumbering and, of course, forests. So the place lends to art made with wood, not to mention with turkey feathers and the antlers of elk and deer. Leonard and fellow Potter County carvers—many of whom remain—have been known for years as the Allegheny Carvers, a club whose living members meet to share and compare work, and to occasionally demonstrate at community events.

Leonard Treat's method was reductive. When his daughter, Rhoda Treat Weimer, asked one time how he managed to carve such an exquisite lady, he responded, "You cut off everything that doesn't belong on a woman." You can't help but think of the method of Ernest Hemingway and Michelangelo Buonarroti. Not bad company for an obscure northern Appalachia artist.

This makes me think of an important lesson I learned in undergraduate school, courtesy of a not-so-obscure northern Appalachia visual artist named Chuck Olson. I was taking a required photography class at St. Francis College. We journalism majors were interested in photography as communication, not as art, sure each of us were in line to be the next Nellie Bly or Jimmy Breslin. But our instructor was an art teacher, and he'd be damned if we weren't going to learn the art of photography. I've been thankful for that since, for on the first day of class, Professor Olson made clear how art did not fit conventional notions of progress. The paintings of the cave dwellers, he made us understand, were no better or worse than those of the aforesaid Michelangelo.

Here in northern Appalachia, we bear witness to what Professor Olson taught. Not that we're indignant cave dwellers. Instead, we appreciate that Emily Dickinson was not the only secretive woman to compose profound poetry in a small-town attic. We respect the chainsaw as a legitimate tool in sculpture, the turkey feather as a suitable canvas, and spoons as musical instruments. Our conditions have conditioned us to the purest conception of art. Democratically, we understand that the sculptures of Leonard Treat, like the work of the fine writers you will experience in the pages that follow, are as worthy as those of celebrated masters from cities that have little in common with Crooksville, Ohio; Vienna, West Virginia; or Schnellsburg, Pennsylvania. The Northern Appalachia Review continues to awaken the world to that reality.

PJ Piccirillo
Founding Editor
Editor-in-Chief

Be Grounded

You will be involved one day,
in the relaxed cadence of conversation,
when suddenly that meek voice
that always challenged your tongue's
authenticity, is quiet. It will be clear
to you unexpectedly that you escaped
your rustic phonetic norms and values:
you won admission to a non-exclusive
club at the expense of your birthright.
And you will realize no one was waiting
for you or looking forward to you embracing
their traditions in Brahman elocution,
their methods of framing the world,
their vanguard of knowledge.
Your presence was always expected,
not required. Your acceptance—token.
And when the brogue of your rearing
breaks through in moments of emotive
speech, they will look at you
with amusement or disdain,
asking only where you're from
or why you're here. And when
you blush with disgrace,
feeling somehow beneath them,
and apologize for those you left
fanning the original voice of your
self-nature, those you admire
will not care. They will know
you have hidden your place

with its minor caste of caricatures,
which sets you apart from them.
It is only a strong grounding
and rooted clarity, unabashed,
that no one can challenge. Don't hide.
When your light is shining
and you feel obliged to change,
tell yourself: "This is who I am."
A secure foundation will cure
around you. The cardinal will sing
its two-part melody: cheer, cheer.

Sorting

I dropped my first piece of fine china,
a Limoges cup with a pattern of roses,
at a tea party on my mother's hardwood floor
in her ice-blue dining room.

The second time I broke something valuable?
It was a cranberry
glass bowl filled with truffles.
I turned too fast, hurrying
to answer the doorbell:
the police had arrived to tell us all about the accident.

I had not thought of my father breaking—
he was not china, not glass. Instead,
he was made of muscle and bone,
thoughts and ideas.

* * *

I tried to pick up the pieces of my mother's heart
and pretended mine was not broken—
that mine was made of metal,
or maybe the dark purple stone
of the Alleghenies—
I knew that metal doesn't break
the way china and glass do;
that was a truth and a lie.

Metal snaps and has sharp edges.
Metal vehicles crash and split open.
And when they do,
people often snap and split open too.
They do.

* * *

Things. There were things all around us:
antique furniture, dishes, tables, tools,
a few electronic devices, magazines,
and piles and piles of books.

The first thing my mother gave
away were all my father's books:
378 of them. It was my job
to sort them shelf after shelf,
pile after pile—
I threw them into large cardboard boxes
on a hot summer day in the back yard—
tasting sweat and salty tears,
smelling bears and blueberries.

* * *

Decades have passed, and I wrestle
with who I was, who I have been, and who I am,
and of course, who I am still becoming—
sorting myself memory by memory,
day by day, word by word.

Yearlings

Our motion-detecting camera captures
    a yearling deer at 2:06 a.m. In the grainy
black and white clip, he takes tentative steps

on our square of lawn: circus performer
    on stilts, wobbly piñata. Ears like two blades
of a ceiling fan, rear legs splayed,

knobby as the spindles of an upright Steinway.
    I read once that Victorians draped piano legs
because they were too titillating.

[*Look it up,* I would tell a student
    writing this poem.] What was I dreaming about
at that moment? Most likely

the election, how the president
    turned all our televisions black. We reached
into our empty screens to retrieve armfuls

of darkness. In class this week we read a poem
    in which the speaker compared school buses
to goldfish in a stream. *What came first,*

a young woman asked, *the buses or the fish?*
    This semester my students are a Brady Bunch
grid of faces, our class *remote* due to the pandemic.

They are taking their first steps into poetry.
    You've gotta crawl before you can walk,
people say. But my own children

never crawled. They sat like small Buddhas
    till they were almost fourteen months old,
then went straight to toddling.

It's late October. Every day I see bodies
    of deer smeared across I-99—
bloody and disemboweled, entrails rutted

by tire tracks. Sometimes one seems
    to be sleeping on the shoulder, no visible sign
of injury—clipped, no doubt, internal bleeding.

[Here's where I'd say read William Stafford:
    I thought hard for us all—my only swerving—,
then pushed her over the edge into the river.]

Hundreds of migrant children may never
    see their parents again. *Unreachable,*
our government deems them.

The yearling sniffs the sideview mirror
    of my car, then startles, as if
his name has just been called.

He leaves a brushstroke in his wake
    like breath against cold night air.
I think hard for us all.

In Dutch

He snapped
off a lilac

switch

and didn't quit

till my sandals

spit
blood.

Waist High

When you were just waist high,
up to the buckle, you ran with
the neighborhood hooligans, until
one girl launched a heavy river rock
at you, and knocked you down, and then, she
toppled you until you admitted it,
under a gush of river water, a confession:
that you wanted to be a girl. She knocked
out your tooth and it dug into your palm,
as you held it like a pearly gate door,
partially rotten. You brought it home
as proof of what all the kids knew, all along.
You were small for your age, a boy who wanted
nothing more than to be a girl.
You had valley shadow deep blues
under your eyes, your eyes double
hung like windows, and you viewed the world
differently, somewhat upside down like a valley
on the floor of two ridges. Two directions, home
and back, took you past the mean girl's house, who
haphazardly hissed her words, and her blue eyes
squinted under hair tangled into coppery
lights. *There's a copperhead,* she warned, *lying
in my driveway, sunning itself, and I'll whip you
with it if you cross my path.* You ventured
a guess that she was telling the truth.
You knew she was just another hungry belly to feed
at her house, and she was bullied, too.
You knew enough to run past her when you

saw the ugly sneer on her face. You were
yeigh high, and about as much tall, and wise
to her ways. She was beaten down, too,
so she got so high, one day, that she fell,
tripping against the Court Street brick.
She had two black eyes, and eye
lashes guarding keenly hidden sadness,
and you just wanted to join her, to put on
lipstick and roll a skirt to show
that you, too, had running legs.

Something Terrible and Beautiful

Something both terrible and beautiful beckoned Vergil Paxton down the country lane. He had awakened at 6 a.m., which meant he already was late for his meeting with Corny Campbell. He shouldn't be late—couldn't be late—not today.

Friday's rain followed by Saturday's hot sun caused the dirt road to be rutted and cracked. Tracing the most direct route, Vergil ran along the ruts as long as he could until he came to a mountain of clay, and he zigzagged around the clumps. The ten-year-old wore a pair of boots that had been his brother Stevie's. Stevie had left home to join the Navy a year earlier, and despite an extra pair of socks, his feet slid inside the boots. They already hurt from sliding around in oversized shoes. Despite the discomfort and the awakening sense of fear, Vergil pushed on.

"Vergil, wait up. Come on. I can't walk as fast as you," yelled Vergil's six-year-old brother, Melvin, who trailed about fifty feet behind. Melvin had bothered Vergil since the moment he left the house. Then the thought occurred to him that his brother had bothered him from the moment he was born. He needed to do something about his brother. Vergil had toyed with the idea of luring Melvin into an open freight car bound for California and waving goodbye as the train pulled away. It was either that or beat him from time to time.

"Go home. Go back to the house. I told you to get lost. Scram." Vergil yelled over his shoulder, but Melvin ignored his orders and jogged to keep up.

Vergil lowered his head and began to run faster. He was a pretty good runner, and he knew he could outrun his brother. Vergil ran past a barn with a "Dewey for President" sign painted on it. An older "Chew Mail Pouch Tobacco" sign bled through the Dewey sign, making it look like a "Dewey for Tobacco" sign.

From a distance, Melvin shouted, "I'm telling Ma and Pa. If you won't let me see this, I'll make sure you don't either."

Vergil considered his brother's threat. He had no doubt Melvin would tattle on him. He wondered if he'd be able to see what Corny was going to show him before his Pa snatched him out of the house. He knew Pa would whup him, too. The question was, would it be worth it?

Maybe.

On the one hand, Corny promised to show him something that would be about the most fantastic thing he'd ever seen. Corny'd whispered about it in school for the final weeks before the summer break about how much fun it was. After school let out, several of the boys had talked about it constantly. A week earlier, a pile of their classmates had showed up at Corny's house to see it, but Corny's Ma had been there, and they had to make an excuse about being thirsty. The other day, Corny, Vergil and a couple of other kids snuck into the house when his Ma was out, but after much effort and sweat, Corny couldn't make it work. He announced it would only work first thing in the morning. That's when you could be sure to see it. The anticipation ate at Vergil.

On the other hand, Corny was a big talker. Most recently, he had bragged about the new shotgun his father had bought at an auction. "It's the biggest shotgun in Bradford County," Corny boasted.

Vergil and some of the other boys from the class hurried to the house after school to see it. Corny opened the lower drawers, then climbed up onto his father's dresser, got the key out of the top drawer, then opened the closet in which the gun had been stowed against the back wall. He brought it out and marched with it like a soldier in the Army. Just like his big brother, PFC Luther C. Campbell, in Patton's Second Armored Division, he said. Vergil could see right away that the shotgun was no larger than his Pa's. It was pretty standard, maybe even smaller. He knew Stevie would call it "regulation." No big deal.

The only thing different about it was that Vergil saw right away that it was loaded. Vergil's Pa never left a shotgun or any other weapon lying around the house loaded. What a talker.

Nevertheless, plans were made, and the boys agreed that on Sunday, at 6 a.m., they would gather in the Campbell's kitchen to see the weird stuff Corny had promised. Vergil ached with anticipation. He'd wanted to see this since he'd first heard about it. The only problem was, Melvin could screw it all up. Vergil stopped in his tracks.

He turned and watched Melvin as he slowly approached. Vergil had outrun his brother and Melvin was about spent. Sweat soaked his shirt and his small face was dirty.

"Why are you so mean to me?" Melvin looked down.

"Why are you such a pest?"

Vergil shook his head then said, "Were you really gonna tell Pa?"

"If I had to. I want to see this too. If I can't, you shouldn't be able to see it either."

"All right, you can come, but you'll have to stand in the back with the other kids and keep quiet. Corny said no brothers or sisters, but he'll have to make an exception."

The Campbell house was old and ramshackle, even by Washington Township standards. Two oak trees stood guard in the front yard on either side of the walk and leaves from the fall still littered the yard. The house was brick and Vergil wondered how Corny got his initials, CCC, and the number 1814 into the brick chimney above the house. Any wood siding on the house hadn't seen the wet end of a paintbrush in years, probably decades. In front of the house, rhododendron bushes had grown to monster size. Where grass grew at all, it was kept low only because the family's animals kept it trim. The only thing that seemed to work was the fence and gate, and even Vergil knew without the fence, the Campbells' animals would wander off.

Corny opened the door even before the boys could knock. He held his finger up against his lips, *keep quiet*, then motioned the boys with his finger. He wore coveralls and a tattered shirt. No shoes. None of the Campbell children, there were eight of them, wore shoes in the summer.

"Why'd you bring him?" Corny whispered loudly pointing at Melvin.

"He followed me. Said he'd tattle on us."

Vergil looked around. "Where are the other kids? I thought you said dozens of kids would be here for this?"

Corny shrugged. "Well, we've got to do this now. Ma will be up soon and once she gets up, it's game over."

Corny leaned against the warped wooden counter near the sink. Clean dishes were stacked in piles on either side of the sink on top of a towel and the only sound was from chickens clucking in the yard through the open window. Vergil and Melvin got up close to Corny.

"Give me some room, will ya?"

They backed up a few inches.

Thinking back on Corny's previous exaggerations, Vergil said, "Well, are you gonna show us?"

"Sure, let me get started."

Corny plunged his hands deep into his pockets. He closed his eyes and fumbled for many seconds and Vergil wondered how long he was going to stall. Finally, Corny pulled out a matchbook and laid it on the counter near the sink. Then, he produced a flint lighter, like Pa used for welding. Finally, he grabbed a box of kitchen matches from the cabinet near the Floyd's Garage Calendar which hung on the wall, the days crossed off on the June 1944 page.

"So how does this work?" Vergil asked. "I mean what do you have to do?"

"I saw my cousin do this. He said the best time is in the morning. I know Ma finished doing the dishes last night around eight. That means the gas has built up for over ten hours. We only get one chance. Once we open the faucet the gas'll come out with the water and then we have to wait until tomorrow morning to try again. My cousin said the flint lighter was the safest way to go. But, I don't know, it ain't easy to get a spark out of that thing."

Vergil picked up the pack of matches. His Pa and Ma had these for their cigarettes. He looked at the cover, it read, "Roosevelt for President."

"Pa says Roosevelt is a Commie. Where'd you get these Commie matches?" Vergil asked.

Corny shrugged. "If you don't like the matchbook, let's just use the kitchen matches. They work real good and will hold a flame for a lot longer than that matchbook."

Corny picked up the box of kitchen matches and pulled out one of the matches. Then, as if on second thought, he pulled out a half-dozen matches and clumped them together like a torch. "We only get one chance till tomorrow. Let's make sure we have enough fire."

Vergil looked at his brother who had squeezed in between himself and Corny. "You sure this is safe? I mean, I know it's water and all, but when you light it on fire, won't there be an explosion? Maybe it'll blow up the house, us and all?" Vergil gestured around the kitchen.

"Sure, it's safe. I've seen my cousin do this lots of times. It makes a pop and then the water will be on fire for a couple of seconds. Then the water puts itself out. It's perfectly safe."

Footsteps from upstairs creaked through the ceiling. The boys froze, then looked toward the stairway.

"Shoot. Ma will be down here in a couple of minutes." Corny took the matches and was about to strike the box when he handed the matches to Vergil. "Here, you have the honors."

Vergil held the matches, but his hands started to shake. "I, I can't." He looked at his brother, then smiled. "Here Mel, you do it." He put the clump of matches into Melvin's filthy hand and gave him the matchbox.

"Sure, but I can't reach. I can't reach the water."

Vergil grabbed his brother by the waist and held him against the sink so his little hand could reach the water. Corny put his hand on the faucet.

"I'll turn on the water, but only after you have a flame," Corny said. "Don't put the fire into the water, just near it. Okay?"

Melvin struck the matches against the box. Nothing happened. He struck them again. Nothing. Then, a moment later, one of the matches ignited and the tips of all the matches caught fire and emitted a sulfurous flame. The boys all looked at the torch. Vergil and Melvin looked at Corny. He smacked his dry lips together and turned the faucet so it was fully open.

Nothing came out. Deep beneath the house, a pipe rattled, and a noise rumbled from the well. The spigot made a low hiss. Vergil nodded at his brother who held the match torch close to the spigot. Nothing happened. Suddenly, the flame popped ever so slightly. Just a single "pop" like a soap bubble bursting. A whisper of disappointment.

Vergil looked at Corny who shrugged. He was about to lower his brother, when unexpectedly, water shot out of the pipe. As the water gurgled maliciously, the tip of the flame, which had pointed to the ceiling, turned sideways and was drawn toward the stream of water. No one had a chance to react.

WHUMP!

The noise was louder than the backfire from Mr. Rankin's old Model T pickup truck. The boys were all thrown onto the floor. Everything in the kitchen shook violently. Some old dishes Mrs. Campbell displayed on top of a cabinet crashed to the floor and shattered into thousands of pieces. The Floyd's Garage calendar fluttered from the wall. For an instant, Vergil saw a blue flame arc around the kitchen before it turned yellow, then orange, then it disappeared.

From upstairs Mr. Campbell screamed, "What the heck? Cornelius Campbell, what the heck is going on?"

Mrs. Campbell shrieked, and the dog started to bark.

A baby began crying and a child yelled, "Mama?"

Outside, the animals made every conceivable noise known to those animals, and then some.

Vergil was back on his feet; his head hurt from where it had hit the wooden floor. His brother staggered around the room holding his face. Corny ran in a circle with his hands to his ears. Brown water sprayed from the faucet. Vergil grabbed his brother's hand. The three boys hit the kitchen door at the same moment, struggled, and then were violently expelled from the house and fell down the step into the yard. Vergil quickly looked at the house and saw smoke coming from the kitchen window. He gripped Melvin's hand harder and began to run. Corny ran in the opposite direction.

Vergil did not let go of Melvin until they were nearly home, about a half mile from the Campbell house. He stopped running and bent over to catch his breath. A high-pitched noise rang in his ears, and everything sounded muffled.

"Melvin, Mel? Are you okay?" Vergil doubled over, panted, and gasped for breath.

He looked at his brother. His face was blackened with soot. His eyelashes, eyebrows and much of the hair at the front of his head had disappeared. Melvin's pants were soaked, he had peed himself. Vergil felt sorry for his brother who had taken the brunt of the explosion, since his face was the closest to the water when the built-up gas blew. From his brother's expression, he couldn't tell if he was going to cry, throw up, or what. Tears began streaming down Vergil's face as the fear caught up with him and he worried about what his parents would do when they saw Melvin.

Suddenly, Melvin's eyes widened. They looked large next to his soot-covered skin. He broke into a wide grin and then let go with an irrepressible laugh.

"Let's do it again."

The Farmer's Son and Daughter

went off to college,
traded in their diplomas
for tickets to the city
and only return for Xmas
and funerals.

At wakes they sit
in the basement of the church,
folded into chairs that
no longer
fit the contours of their lives.
Sampling potato salad,
sipping warm coffee
with powdered creamer
from styrofoam cups
balanced upon their knees,

they nod politely as old men
eulogize their late father with stories
of getting lost on coon-hunt nights
and the time
the brakes gave out on Joe Pye Hill
and he yelled, "Bail out, boys!"—
just in the nick of time.

After the funeral, they walk the farm
with the land developer, agreeing
as they shake hands and seal the deal
that yes indeedy, the fresh country air,

peace and quiet
and gently rolling hills are lovely—
with good drainage and percolation,
and that once the county roads are
improved to make daily commutes
to and from the city manageable,
the subdivision
will be a lovely place to raise children,
and maybe the yuppies can keep a hen
or two—
if the building codes allow.

Blues in the Winter

"Just don't offer him anything to drink.
He can come to play music, but he's 20,
underage, the kind of kid that if friends
say walk to the corner, he'll stop everything
and go, or worse. Know what I mean?"
says his father. And I say, yes—
because I do know,
and have wished that this father,
my friend, would ask me to walk
to the corner, or worse.

And so Robert Jr. blows in
like a blizzard, a Gibson Firebird
and a fifth of Wild Turkey,
his dad's good looks, but eyes
that burn bluer, hair that shines blacker,
a kid who channels Stevie Ray,
Johnny Winter, and he offers me
his whiskey, and I drink in each shot
of courage, find a chance to allow
my harp to sing back.

His fingers spin and slide,
race and dance down the neck
of his guitar, hitting notes
that just get started
where normally notes might end,
and this is where this story ends,
not about the boy, not about the dad,

who stayed my friend, a good man,
but about the music, about the blues,
and how ice forms around the edges
of each grief and sorrow,
how just the right notes can find
all the empty places on the skin,
how this is where the fire gets in.

I Am From

Inspired by George Ella Lyon's "Where I'm From"

I am from cinders tracked in by careless feet, from Ivory soap well lathered and applied before a crackling fireplace during winter wash-pan baths.

I am from the house on Main Street, dingy white siding, a cement stoop too high for short legs.

I am from tomato plants hanging full of fruit destined for Mason jars, morning glory blossoms sporting ballerina skirts in red and pink and purple, a peach tree limb perfect for climbing, and weeping willow fronds that sweep and sway with each breath of summer.

I am from a house divided—his family, her family—the child too much her to fit his, too much him to fit hers, antipodes in mindset; in reality, a one-sided coin.

I am from my father's mother, who quoted, "Whistling girls and crowing hens always come to some bad end," as she went about her day boldly whistling. From my mother's mother, who feared the worst, a crepe hanger of the highest order.

I am from "Quitters never win and winners never quit" and "You may not be pretty, but you do look smart."

I am from slick wooden pews and long sermons, from discovering syllabication by connecting breaks in hymnal lyrics to the spacing of notes, from a mother who tempered the most austere teachings with grace and humanity.

I am from the banks of the Muskingum River, from a mixture of Scots and Irish and English and French. I am from the peasant fare they passed along: potatoes boiled in their jackets topped with chopped onion and drizzled with bacon fat, pinto beans swimming in broth where ribbons of smoked jowl rind wiggled like worms.

I am from the Frenchman who fled Paris for Ireland just before the Saint Bartholomew Day Massacre slaughtered his fellow Huguenots, and the Scot who arrived in Watertown, Ohio, commissioned to build a grist mill, who carved out a home on Muddy Branch and had a go at the English in 1812.

I am from dusty albums of sepia prints in which unsmiling women in corsets pose beside men whose celluloid collars stretch their necks like nooses. From their storage crocks, jugs, pottery spittoons and bean jars that peep from corners and hover beneath tables. From one grandmother's egg basket and the other's thimble, practical things passed along, bearing their stories and their spirit.

Control

Here's my brother, again,
with my father's smile
the one that he flickered on
when he had to, when
he wanted others to
almost like him, say, when he
finally stopped to ask for
directions and made a joke
out of it, *I can speak to them*
in their own language,
he'd say, pulling into some
gas station out in the country,
where men wore bib overalls smudged
from labor as strange to him as roads
that led us to where we
all wished we weren't, and now
that smile shows up, thin
and grim, keeping a lid on
but soon to boil over if some car
in front had left its blinker flashing,
or hung out in the passing lane
but didn't drive fast enough,
or someone honked, *So*
your horn works, now try your
lights, white knuckles on the wheel,
foot on the accelerator, and after
the first time it wasn't
that funny, and now
my brother's body isn't his own,

Dad's uninvited ghost
barges back, not a hint
of regret, no way to know
how to deal with it,
now it's drawing a map
on my brother's lips, that road
between slapstick and slap,
sucker and punch, in control
and out of it.

Jessica Cory

Life in the Time of COVID: A Stresstina

Adjusting my mask,
I head into the store,
careful to sanitize
the cart, my hands.
Now the 'new normal'
in these 'unprecedented times.'

In these/End these times
I've learned vodka can mask
loneliness, make you appear normal.
But it's unsustainable to store
depression in idle hands,
even if they're sanitized.

The difference b/t insanity and insanitized
is the amount of time
I sit staring at my hands.
Noticing how the thin skin masks
ligaments, cells, muscle memories stored,
how these musings are 'abnormal.'

But, then again, 'normal'
is defined in the DSM's sanitized
terms, checkboxes that store
themselves in the before-times:
pre-vent talk, pre-distancing, pre-masks.
When our fates were in the hands

of God (or maybe even ourselves), not the hands
of checkout clerks, restaurant workers, normal
everyday people, now heroes unmasked
(or should it be 'masked')? Either way, they sanitize
their spaces a million times
a day, hoping to restore

a sense of safety. But what's in store,
we can't know. The fate lines on my hands
have deepened since the last time
I gazed at them. But I don't know what normal
fate lines look like. Maybe all the sanitizer
is to blame. How deep are fate lines unmasked?

In the before-times, I felt normal.
Now I'm distant, sanitized.

My hands are where I store my masks.

The Laughing Opossum

My backyard faces a wild, wooded bank that slips down to a stream into a small mountain thick with trees. During winter, I often leave crusts of bread for the squirrels at the base of a pine tree. On this night, I had the remains of a slice of toast, but I shivered in the furious snow squall and tossed it quickly on the back porch and slammed the door against the storm. Even the squirrels were too cold to run up on the porch and eat it. But an opossum was hungry.

When I flicked on the outside light, we both froze at the sight of each other. The opossum is built like a bullet—pointy snout and head, almost streamlined, leading back to an oval body with silver-tipped fur. Rows of sharp little teeth in her V-shaped mouth, and black-fingered paws hold the bread for her to bite.

She was kind of a mess, though, as vicious vermin go. Something had taken a chunk out of her back and scraped her raw. Her tail was only a few inches long and kinked in the middle, as if it had been folded in half. Part of one ear was missing, too. I had just read, in the coincidence-but-not-really- way, that during sub-zero cold snaps, opossums can lose tails, ears, and toes to frostbite. And it had been wickedly cold here for too many days in a row.

An abundance of wildlife prevails in my rural northeastern Pennsylvania town. Deer, raccoons, and misplaced college students are all part of the landscape. They seek the same sustenance: food, shelter, and alcohol. When a buck finds fermented apples, the party is on. I teach college students while also learning from them. Any teacher who doesn't acknowledge that education is a two-way street has definitely been in the woods with said fermented apples.

Then spring break brought a virus that would force isolation and overcrowding upon all of us. This is when the world learned to spell "quarantine." This is when the connections started to unravel and engagement tanked. Non-verbal communication adds greatly to expression; a student promising to turn in an assignment while slouched in a chair staring at the ground is a cry for help that a teacher can support. But with technology, everyone sits still, framed by their own square of video, and sometimes even that is blank with just a haunted voice rising out of a black box. If I can make them laugh now, my lost students, it might be the one part of the day where they don't have to think about their grades, their futures, their optional wearing of pants.

So, I brought the opossum to school.

I named her Poosséy and posted video of her dinnertime to class. There were astonished smiles and notes of concern as to my mental health. But this redirection of focus gave them a break from the seriousness of praying for good Wi-Fi with clear audio and real-time video. Where did she come from? Where does she go when she scurries away? Poosséy has a freedom we humans lack.

Through the following weeks, we talk about her preference for mangoes, her impeccable face washing, and her patchy fur. Poosséy has opened the class to a new level of interaction, and we have discussions about the opossum. The students bring me caring suggestions for a struggling creature, with a sense of control at a time when we have none.

Last night Poosséy laughed. It is getting warmer, and I can hear her through the screen door. After a feast of French fries, she lifted her bullet-shaped head, pointy teeth bared in a smile and waggled her whole body. Her fur is growing back nicely, and her ear has healed. Her tail remains short and crooked, however. Some things will never be the same, in the way this virus has infected us all.

The semester is almost over. The students are ensconced in final exams, bursting into their future dreams. Poosséy does not come every night now, as it is getting warmer, and someone has to eat all those delicious ticks. All my wildlife will scamper away at the same time, plump and moonstruck, just as nature intended.

First Trip

Nuisance rain dotted the windshield through West
Virginia, wipers on, wipers off, clouds hovered
close to mountaintops, but Maryland
opened skies to cumulus rabbit ears
popped and listening. Cicadas roared
at a rest stop, and soon windows powered
up, wipers swishing splattered bugs.

By Pennsylvania, heat hit, and orange barrels
lined the lanes. Semis squealed brakes, cars
slowed, traffic built, crept. I took a turn, let
GPS have its way through small towns with
old stone and brick, unchained hotels, and family
diners. Every corner offered ice cream.
I needed a bathroom more.

With Covid, every stop seems dangerous.
Mask, no mask. Travelers smile, but eye each
other warily. Alone too long, I'm watchful,
others toss caution away like a bee-filled can.
We venture out, try to remember old ways.
When I arrive, I will need a hug.
Will I ever arrive the same?

April, Masks and Morels

I do not know how to sew,
but I have been sewing surgical masks.
It is not hard to do, though my fingers
are stiff and my stitches uneven.

Each action takes attention,
points my brain into a sharp focus,
a stitch, an eighth of an inch,
and then the next one.

In the same way, I hunt for morels,
though I am awkward in the deep woods,
stumble over tangled branches,
snag my pants. I scan slantwise,

and sometimes they materialize,
each honeycombed cap reminding me
that hunting is part of finding,
that my desire should not exceed

my patience. I step cautiously,
narrow my gaze, grateful for
small things in springtime, how they
help keep the weary world at bay.

Finding My Way

My feet pound the pavement and I run, kicking up dust and gravel and breathing in air that gives me life despite its pollution from defunct steel mills.

I run past homes that floodwaters didn't quite destroy but made uninhabitable, structures slowly decaying with broken windows and dilapidated steps that lead to sagging porches.

Finding my stride, I run over the bridge of the Stonycreek River that raged in the floods of 1889, 1936, and recently, in 1977, now calm, meandering slowly without a hint of potential destruction.

Running through potholed streets to familiar sidewalks, I return to my neighborhood and nosy neighbors who peer at me, parting lace-trimmed curtains, not offering a thumbs up but a scowl.

Heart pounding and fists pumping, I continue past my house. I run away. I want to leave, but I have nowhere to go.

* * *

In my teen years, I wanted to figure out how to be anywhere other than where I was living. I wanted to run away.

I saw people, mostly men, but sometimes men and women walking the railroad tracks in my neighborhood. I wondered if that was a way I could just disappear, set out on the tracks and be taken somewhere else. Anywhere else.

I wanted to be anywhere but in my home with the never-ending drama of addiction. Constant conflict built up between my mother and stepfather that spilled into all the relationships in our household.

Our home, located in the 8th Ward of the city of Johnstown, was a tall, narrow, brick house with lots of small rooms and low ceilings.

The tiny rooms in our home were filled with furniture, knick-knacks, a floor-model stereo and record albums, a series of encyclopedias, and my mother's Harlequin romance books. There was a basement where we roller-skated and one staircase leading to the second floor that had a den, a sewing room, and my favorite part of the house, a hallway that connected the sewing room and the third-floor stairway.

That hallway seemed unnecessary as an architectural feature, but it held a table with many different rocks, shells, and fossils. This, to me, was the most interesting part of our cluttered home.

This next stairway led to the top floor where my two sisters and I each had our own rooms.

There was no hallway, just one room that led into another room and a bathroom connected to my room, the middle room. We all had fluffy bedspreads and canopies on each of our beds.

We all chose our room colors. My sister Heather, whose room you entered at the top of the stairs, chose mint green with a bright pink trim. I chose bright pink with a vibrant blue trim, and my sister Kelly chose bright yellow. Sometimes children shouldn't be given full agency in these types of situations. Pastel sensory overload.

At night, my sisters and I tried, without success, to sleep. The yelling, the throwing of pots and pans, and the crying traveled up two flights of stairs to our rooms. Laying in my bed, in my stupid room that resembled a baby shower on steroids, I felt trapped, in my pastel nightmare, fists and teeth clenched.

Rage-filled arguments in my room led my mother, or sometimes me, to sweep arms across the surfaces of dressers and vanities, scattering the contents to the floor, throwing clothes out of drawers, breaking valuables to discharge this enormous, volatile exchange in the pink room.

Boundaries fell away in how my stepfather spoke to me about my body—my thin and awkward body that I tried to shrink and make disappear.

He called me "Bones" and would sometimes lurch forward to jab and tickle me, a thinly veiled attempt to grope at my breasts and crotch.

The smallness of the rooms in our home made it awkward and difficult to create space between persons. Anytime I walked past him, I tried to make my body small and to move so quickly to avoid this exchange. Sometimes, this worked; other times, it did not.

* * *

I often thought about ending my life. Once I took half a bottle of aspirin during my period thinking I could just bleed out.

Rather than doing this in my own bed, I decided on a night when my mother and stepfather were away from the house. I chose our living room with its red shag carpet, ceramic bull-fighter figurines on one wall, and decorations my mother had made on another wall, dark brown stained corkboard with a square of the shag rug on it and in the center, attached to the square were items I can only describe as possible instruments of torture from the Spanish Inquisition, a ball with spikes and a sword-like device.

It seemed appropriate.

I took half a bottle of aspirin.

That night, my grandmother sat with us girls, watching old Godzilla movies on our sectional couch. Perhaps I could die a slow, comfortable death, bleeding while watching a giant reptile crushing and destroying humans. I thought my blood could swirl and blend in with the shag carpet, the instruments of torture and the red bull with its menacing horns.

Perhaps, I would dissipate into this scene.

Instead, I bled profusely through many menstrual pads and onto the sectional couch. I felt drowsy, fell asleep, and woke with no one knowing anything other than I bled onto the couch. Probably anemic, I continued to exist.

Finding myself still alive, later that week, I pleaded to live with my dad.

I asked this several times for myself and for my sisters.

No. The answer each time we asked.

No.

My mother sat on our couch underneath the Spanish Inquisition instruments and wept and also denied this request.

At the time, my dad and stepmother tended to my grandfather who was incapacitated by a stroke. They also fostered three young girls, who they eventually adopted.

But my dad never inquired deeply into our asking.

*   *   *

We were a working-class family in a blue-collar steel town in the late 1970s/early 1980s. I didn't know anyone who had had therapy or counseling, and it was never offered to me. Watching Phil Donahue was the closest anyone in my family ventured towards therapy.

I walked through the halls in my school, sat at desks, did my schoolwork, went to church and Sunday school; all the while I was a churning ball of pain. It seemed so obvious to me that I was damaged, different, and suffering. I hoped that maybe my school counselor or church elder or pastor would be able to see the horrible pain I was in. No one noticed. And I didn't know I could, or that I had the right to, ask for help.

I couldn't stand to be in my own skin. I didn't necessarily want to die, but I could not bear the pain. I didn't know what else to do.

So, I started running.

One unseasonably warm day in gym class during my sophomore year, we were given permission to run or walk around the track.

Gym was my least favorite class. I frequently ducked away from balls hurtling towards me and I was generally one of the last picks for team sports.

However, this day, the bright sky, the chill with a promise of warmth, the freedom to decide how to move around the track, something, maybe grace, inspired me to run. I found a rhythm and breathed through the stitch in my side and ran around the track that had one side facing the river wall. I ran breathing in the faint fumes of sulfur from acid mine drainage. I pumped my arms, hands in fists while my long legs found their stride. I felt euphoric and free in the wide-open spaces where a fresh slice of heaven had just been revealed to me that day.

Needing and wanting more of this feeling, I joined my high school track team.

It was extremely uncharacteristic of me to do anything athletic as the nerdy, awkward, trombone-playing girl, and none of the few friends I had at the time had this interest. I was never very competitive.

My first track meet was at Westmont Hilltop Middle School Track. Girls and Boys ran the mile together. We all lined up for the race.

The starting gun went off. Everyone took off at a pace far faster than mine. I ended up lapped and coming in dead last, but I didn't give up. I ran and finished my first race while some lingered to watch my lone figure reach the finish line.

I heard laughter and shouts and assumed I was being made fun of. Years later, one of the girls on the team corrected me, sharing that they cheered for me because I refused to give up. I didn't know it was an option.

Looking at this now, I have renewed respect for my younger self. That young self who was deeply cloaked in shame, blame, resentment. That younger self who felt stuck, frozen, numb, until she started running.

That younger self found she loved feeling the intensity of moving fast, of pounding her feet on the pavement, the sound of the gravel underneath her feet on the high school track.

When I started to run, muscles in my arms and legs began to emerge.

Finding a rhythm to my pace and linking it to my breath brought a smile to my face and allowed me to experience and embody joy.

My body! My body, sweat running down the small of my back, my body feeling free and strong.

My body, making choices and having agency.

My body.

Mine.

When I ran through the first level of fatigue, sheer exhilaration was on the other side. I had no idea this existed and that I could summon it myself.

When I ran, the voices in my head that questioned my existence vanished.

So, I ran through my neighborhood of the 8th Ward, past the train tracks, Moxham and Hornerstown, on streets and sidewalks. I ran past industrial buildings, past homes that retained beautiful architecture and spoke of grander times. I ran past homes abandoned after the 1977 flood.

I ran alongside the Conemaugh River whose basin overflowed and destroyed everything in its wake. I ran past the cemetery with unearthed gravestones.

I ran up the vertical DuPont Street, sprinting and gasping for oxygen, passing the neatly kept apartment of my grandmother.

I ran around the high school track with its crunchy gravel and view of the river wall that students regularly tagged with graffiti to proclaim their love.

I ran in the woods on the University of Pittsburgh, Johnstown Campus Nature Trails, snapping leaves and twigs and inhaling peace.

I ran to and from my brick house with plastic flowers on the porch, my house with small rooms, narrow staircases, and low ceilings into the wide-open spaces of the streets.

I didn't run fast, but I ran far.

Running, I learned something about myself.

I had endurance. I didn't have to run away.

I could just *RUN!*

I could be in my body and not want to die.

St. Joseph's Foundlings Home and Maternity Hospital

If you could travel back in time, you might see yourself there: an infant in a metal crib, your small fingers reaching out to curl around its cool slats, intrigued by the sensation. You will be a wide-eyed child who'll see the world with its malevolence and grace and take your place in the middle. Here the Sisters float like saints or daemons in white tunics and headdresses. The leather soles of their shoes slide and tap on polished tile the color of dried blood as they circulate between the rows. It was not a peculiarly busy year. The oldest nuns remember far busier times during the war. Boys shipping out and girls conceding to murmured promises. And the years before the war when things were scarce; another mouth might topple an already too full cart. In early summer, with the windows of the second-floor nursery open, a Sister-nurse might pick you up, hold you in the sunlight and consider: you are a peculiar child in this foundering hard-coal city of Slavs and Italians in an orphan's home run by the donated Irish daughters from around the diocese: a black-haired, brown-skin boy delivered by a woman with a German name and no explanation at all.

G.A.R.

As your mother digs her paltry garden at the foot of the yard in your latest rented house, the metal of her shovel strikes something solid. You phone your buddy to come over. Though you are high school kids, athletes in good shape, it takes the better part of an hour to dig out the large smooth stone which turns out to be a tombstone for a Grand Army of the Republic veteran. At your mother's direction, you wheelbarrow it over to the house, place it face down, use it as a final back porch step for the rest of the time you live there. It never bothers you that there is a dead man buried in the yard next to where you park the car. You walk over him nearly every day. You only wonder what he's been doing there these past hundred years: how he looks, how he feels. There are lots of bodies in this town; it's old and ghosts run free. Or at least that's what you've heard. Ancient men at the Chestnut Inn sometimes argue, their voices betraying faint accents of their Pennsylvania German ancestors, about whether it was two or three haunts who roamed the top floor of the old Neff Hotel right up until it was torn down years back. At recess, kids stand around on blacktop schoolyards and talk about the hermit up on White's Hill who died before they were born: his body found frozen one January, his spirit still restless in the woods that thicken past the creek. You think it all Halloween stuff. Except that one midsummer night just after you graduated school when you walked the derelict railroad bridge. The air was thick with fog and the moon a dulled blur behind it. You stutter stepped the ties, listened to the water gurgle underneath. Halfway across you stopped, lighted a cigarette, then heard voices. Though your pace slowed a bit, you kept going, saw two figures appear, still indistinct only yards away. It was only two stoners who hissed a greeting as they passed, like snakes, more afraid of you than you were of them. On a Sunday, a few nights later, you sat on the back porch of the house, your feet resting on the tombstone step while you drank a beer. You stared over at the back end of a church just up and across the narrow alley. You could hear the preacher preaching the holiness gospel, his voice rising like a threat.

An Appalachian Boy at the Big Eastern School

An Appalachian boy at the big Eastern school—
a boy whose hometown looks to the East,
is closest Midwest, but whose speech, manner
and cognizance bespeaks a trail of mountains
and thick woods of home.

An Appalachian boy at the big Eastern school
wears a flannel shirt, pants never black,
hair only delicately out of place—
and never knows when to say hello, goodbye;
never knows when the season will change,
when the wind will whip up the hill
and scour the bones of the campus.

He's never seen young women so casual
about their dress, yet so careful
that artfully placed exotica
might fall from their ears, so careful
to show an unshaven leg
amid an uneven scent of patchouli.

So carefully he unveils the foreignness
of the place; so carefully he hides
his discoveries, his contentment of knowledge
that comes from the opening of wounds,
the white curtains of light
that break open as he cuts their world
in two, and considers one-half his.

Coaltown Valley Blues, the Almost Happy Life of a Fat Four-Eyed Freak

Working in dirt with Dad, a banjo-pickin' coal-miner, in our hilly backyard rhubarb patch, I paused in the Saturday sun, listening to the lemon whisper of April air pull dandelions from melting coal snow. I was a big-boned girl with thick tortoise-frame glasses. My best friends were the sounds only I could hear.

Dad and Mama called me "special." Joey Kreps, the neighborhood bully and mine owner's son, called me a "fat four-eyed freak." In 1962 nobody in Coaltown Valley, PA had ever heard of synesthesia.

Yesterday during noon recess Joey sidled up, snatched my tin lunch box, dumped my bologna sandwich in the black mud. "Gonna knock you out, freak, next time I see you 'round Floyd's."

Joey lived with his parents in the big house overlooking Floyd's Market where Mama sent me most Saturdays for fresh brown eggs.

"You're daydreaming, Mattie O'Malley," Dad said.

I started crying.

"What's wrong, honey?"

"Joey says he's gonna beat me up if he sees me near Floyd's."

"Forget about Joey. He's all talk."

Dad tossed me an iridescent owl's feather dug from coffee dark dirt, watched me cradle it to my cheek. "Be big-winged," the feather sang, its silver notes tickling my ears.

"You've got the gift, Mattie. Forget Joey." Dad rose slowly, stretched his bony arms, and brushed mud from his frayed flannel shirt.

"The gift, just like old St. Franky here." Dad pointed to our birdbath with its chipped plaster statue of the Saint of Assisi, the saint who spoke the language of birds.

"See those sparrows perched on that old boy's shoulders? Those critters know Franky here is one special cat. Just like you." Dad grinned, happy for a Saturday morning off from twelve hour shifts at the coal mine. "Forget Joey. Think about St. Franky's banjo."

"Tell me again." I never tired of Dad's story. It was not one you'd hear in church.

"One time, before the boy was a saint, robbers waylaid him, beat him up bad. But God sent an angel to play banjo for the poor fella, cheer him up. Music so snappy it chased away the blues. None of those damn harps you see on Christmas cards."

Dad wheezed, then coughed, spitting black gunk. His coughs had grown chainsaw rough over winter, his eyes yellowing more each month.

"Nobody but Franky could hear that angel's banjo. Real dance tune, Franky told folks. Angel left the banjo sounds in Franky's bones before flying away. From then on birds flocked to that boy, perched on his arms and shoulders, safe. Even today folks say you hear heaven when you hear real good pickin'. Banjo's the music of angels, Mattie."

"You hear angels, Dad?"

"Sure do, kiddo." He winked. "Every time your Mama sings."

We both knew Mama couldn't carry a tune. "Screech owl," she called herself. But that never stopped her from singing or laughing at herself.

"Wish I could hear angels pick banjo." I laid my face on the ground. "I only hear snow melt."

He laughed between coughs. "Tell you what, Mattie, forget about old St. Franky's angel. You'll hear heaven's banjos when time's right. For now you listen for the song of coal turning to diamonds. Bet you could hear that. See these old lumps of coal," he picked up two chunks his shovel uncovered, "they turn into diamonds when they've been under terrible pressure for a long, long time."

"Then, man oh man, those diamonds sing. Music'll bowl you over. You know, kiddo, we probably have some singin' diamonds," he pointed to a dark outcropping of coal, "buried in our own backyard."

But I heard nothing.

Dad was back on his knees finishing the rhubarb planting, his thinning copper hair streaked with mud. I squatted down, digging out coal chunks with my spade. I heard only Dad's cough.

Planting done, we walked towards the house, its weathered wooden siding in need of paint. Mama was out front signing for a coal delivery from Allegheny Number 10 Mines, the company where Dad worked.

"Last delivery 'til fall, Miz O'Malley," the driver said. An orange dump truck filled with coal waited in the road. Two workmen waved to Dad then shuttled coal through our cellar transom window. We lived with black dust.

Coal fed the furnace that tried to heat our house through octopus air ducts. Coal fed the potbelly stove in the kitchen, although its warmth didn't quite reach the alcove holding Mama's rhubarb preserves.

"But that's okay," she often said, "my preserves like a little nip in the air."

Dad took Mama and me inside to the kitchen where the metal clothes wringer stood wedged between the icebox and the wash tub.

"I know you been wanting a fancy clothes-washing machine, Rosie, but you deserve a diamond. Happy anniversary, darlin'." He presented her with a tiny diamond ring, having spent their meager savings to surprise her.

"Oh, Earl, you shouldn't have." Worries wrinkled her thick brows.

Dad got his banjo from the closet. "Little rusty, but I'll give it a go, darlin', that tune from the night we met." He started in on "*Cripple Creek*," coughed up more yellow jelly.

"It's okay, Earl, have some pie, rest your bones." She kissed his forehead.

Mama's rhubarb pie was soon on the table, thick with last year's preserves. Her pie tasted like wet caterpillars but I loved the kitchen symphony of Doris Day on the Philco, Mama crooning accompaniment, cheerfully off-key, Dad pickin' banjo despite his coughs.

* * *

Walking to Floyd's through the woods, I hoped to avoid Joey in the early twilight.

"Usual, eh, sweetheart?" Floyd gave me a plump sky-blue popsicle plus a half-dozen eggs warm from his chicken coop.

My lips were stained navy blue before I got out the door. I tried not to think about Joey as I retraced my steps home.

"Well, if it ain't the fat four-eyed freak."

Joey jumped from behind a red oak, hurling a handful of sharp coal nuts at me, knocking the glasses off my face.

Something in the branches above whispered, "Be big-winged." My arms flew out, the eggs flew up. Joey stepped back, tripped over a coal outcropping, fell, hollering, and hit his nose, bleeding into snow, eggs, and popsicle.

I picked up my broken glasses and ran home, eager to report my partial victory to Dad.

An ambulance stood outside our house. Two medics carried Dad on a stretcher.

"Nothing we can do, Miz O'Malley," the Allegheny Hospital doctor declared an hour later.

After the funeral Mama got a job in the mine office. "Company said it's the only way we keep our house."

From then on Mama treated me like the adult I had to become. I forgot about singing diamonds, forgot about angels pickin' banjos. Went to work at Floyd's weekends and evenings. Floyd knew I was only thirteen but real good at floor sweeping. My synesthesia disappeared.

* * *

In the years since Dad died, I got older, got fatter, even got shatterproof glasses, but never got to hear diamonds sing or angels pickin' banjo.

I take care of Mama. I'm all she's got. This afternoon she sat at our Formica kitchen table.

"Don't know where it is. I remember rhubarb."

"Where what is?"

"My diamond, my diamond. Looking at carrots." She slumped down, hands shaking.

That tiny diamond had been on her finger since Dad put it there the day he died.

"At Food-Dollar. Apple bin. Doing this." She slid an imaginary ring up and down her finger, knuckle to nail.

"Has Dad seen my ring?"

I retraced Mama's grocery trip. Looked in the rhubarb, the carrots, in the Red Delicious apples she still got because Dad had loved them. Nothing.

"Has a diamond ring turned up? My Mama lost hers here, she thinks. It's very small."

The produce stocker snorted; the cashier sadly shook her head.

When I got home, I took Mama's hand.

"Wish I could find your diamond." I kissed her fingers. "It hasn't turned up yet." I knew it never would.

Mama sat up straight in her hard ladder-back chair.

"You look a little like my daughter, but she's a good bit younger. Not so fat as you."

"I'm Mattie, Mama."

She tucked a wisp of white hair behind her ear. "You ever heard angels pick banjo? Earl hears 'em all the time, sounds only he hears. Don't tell nobody but me about his gift. Says the mine'd fire him, think him a freak."

She abruptly began to belt out an old favorite as if she were Doris Day reborn wild, atonal, and free.

"*Leave your worries on the doorstep, just direct your feet to the sunny side of the street.*"

She stopped. "Go find Mattie, she knows this song."

"*Just direct your feet,*" I started singing.

Mama joined in, "*To the sunny side of the street.*"

Under cataracts of tears her eyes sparkled. For decades I hadn't heard sounds that only I could hear. But at that moment, in the music of Mama's eyes, I heard diamonds sing.

A rough knock at the front door interrupted us. A scrawny fellow in a dirty Food-Dollar jacket stood on our porch, arms akimbo, nose slightly crooked.

"Mattie? Mattie O'Malley?"

"Joey Kreps?"

"Didn't know you lived here 'til I saw you at the store. I was mean to you as a kid."

"Yes."

"Though you did break my nose." Joey snickered. "I got a heap of making up to do. Let me start by asking you if this here ring is what you're looking for?" My hopes rose. Then he handed me a cheap plastic mood ring. "A shopper found this in the trash, just like your folks, freak." He laughed.

"You piece of shit, you followed me home. Get the hell off my porch."

A week later, I had the nightly news on when KDKA announced Pittsburgh cops had just arrested a Joseph Kreps of Coaltown Valley for jewelry theft. As the crime coverage continued, the damn mood ring, still sitting on the tv table where I had first flung it, turned the colors of burning coal.

Late that night, looking up at the heavens, I thought I heard banjo pickin' in the darkness, whether coming from our old St. Francis bird-bath out back or from a neighbor's porch or from somewhere else far off, I couldn't rightly say. But I heard sounds so snappy they almost chased my blues away—almost but not quite.

Quilting

I learn only what I need from the women.
    —Anon.

The young woman fashions
her days into quilts, stitch by stitch
as her ancestors instruct her.
They crowd around her now
as she works over a quilt frame in the garage,
the only place large enough for it.

There are other quilts behind her
spread out on lines, hanging,
the bright colors she put in them
now dimming in the failing light
of the open garage door.

She pauses and looks up from her work
toward the small blue patch of sky,
but the women draw her back,
gently guide her to listen to them,
stitch just so, follow the patterns.

It is difficult work.
She turns and says,
"It needn't be so big,
so intricate, there are shortcuts."

The old women put their hands up
in horror as she rips the edging
from calico and tosses it down.

Now the angry man is back,
his car in the driveway, idling.
He comes armed with angry words,
angry the door is left open,
angry the quilts are there,
very angry,

but the young woman
doesn't let him drive in.
Day after day the garage
spills over with quilts.

The Doves

The mourning doves
start cooing at dawn,
through the daily news report
of gun violence,
through the phone call
about a friend passing away.

They are cooing up by the eaves,
an initial slide toward brilliance
and then the three low notes,
impeccably spaced. They coo
through the improperly warm
spring afternoon, the early
unfolding of leaves, the siren's wail,
a distant cry.

The next day, there they are
cooing once again, and yet again
throughout the long days of summer,
a steady backdrop of calm on which
we obliviously rely.

Fascination with the Furnace

My imagination always tends to the antiquated. I am inclined to envision what Lewis and Clark feasted their eyes upon during their exploration. I imagined the excitement of Powell's first journey through the canyons. Often, I would pretend to be a burly trapper; no deeds claim the vast beyond. I daydream of old-growth forests, the pristine wilderness the Seneca traversed. My trips down the Allegheny River must still be met with my childlike ability to deconstruct houses, boat docks, and cabins and fill in the blanks with thick greenery.

My fishing and camping trips from my kayak normally end at a dot on the map that holds a steady population of one. This is my grandfather's birthplace, an area he had to leave when the coal mines shut down and they demolished the houses they owned. For the most part, Nature has reclaimed the area. This should be the epitome of my dream! With a conflict of curiosity, I become lost in my grandfather's stories, captivated by the tales of the Allegheny of his youth and struggling to find the context of which he speaks.

Several years before his death, Grandpa, Richard Seybert, was sharing his stories with me as he often did, telling me about living in a few of the surrounding towns before returning to grow up in Sarah Furnace. He stood and walked away, I figured to refill his cup of coffee, but returned instead with a briefcase. Upon opening it, he handed me a large envelope. "If you get tired of my stories, you can feel free to try some of these." I opened the package to find transcripts of old (unspecified) newspaper articles from the area. Most dealt with coal mining operations, feuds and fistfights, family visitors from far away, drownings, church meetings, and successes or problems with the railroads, some articles dating back to the 1800s. This all added to the mystery of the area, such a lively culture for ghost towns.

Six houses still stand on the small road that winds through the mountain near East Brady. My great-uncle, Bill Seybert, owns one of them and uses it as a camp. I visit often and Grandpa's words try to paint a picture. At the end of the road used to stand the tipple, now a gravelly area filled with spent shotgun shells and rifle casings from the neighbors who use the flat as a target range. I cannot see the large lumber building where workers would unload the coal from the mine into large railcars.

I cannot feel the ground shake at one o'clock in the morning from the midnight express. Even in my dreams, I cannot picture the faint lights illuminating weary passengers puffing on cigars through the small windows or see the phantom image of my grandfather as a child standing in the shallows picking soft-shelled crawdads with his father, knowing that this train marks the time to head back home.

A town earns a name of "Furnace" by having a blast furnace that melts down iron ore. I knew only of coal mining, but Grandpa has told me Porter's Caves were made from mining iron ore. Everywhere I now look, I try to deconstruct the oaks and sumac to place simple buildings I have seen in black-and-white or sepia prints. Houses full of workers, permanently pasted graphite grey from years of soot and coal dust. I wonder if my great-grandfather cast an adamantine shimmer from the minerals in his pores if the light hit him right.

My feet start carrying me down the single paved road; the only thing I can still pretend to know is the feeling of when it would have been packed down and rutted only as dirt. Past the creek by our camp stands the foundation of the one-room schoolhouse. My grandfather would rise early and light the coal stove to heat the building in winter. His teacher would give him a small payment in appreciation. I stand for attendance, not even knowing where my desk would be. A tulip poplar has replaced the flagpole, grasses and oak-sprouts the only pupils of a forgotten time. Acorns substitute for the bell, and quaking aspens are the only leaves turning furiously. I can hear the wind coming down the mountain with the murmuring of the creek and can see the currents of the Allegheny. What a grand lecture! Birdsong is the new Alma Mater. Class dismissed. I envy my grandfather's education.

He warned me never to romanticize the area too much, for the toils were great. The town never suffered from the Great Depression, for the area was constantly depressed. The town survived as long as the mine was producing, and, luckily for that town, the war efforts always needed fuel. I come from a generation that has little fear of production, since we get food from grocery stores and produce heat at a flick of a switch. Easy is the life of one on a full belly in a heated home. Since he was a child, his responsibility was filling the coal shed for cooking year-round and heating through the winter months. He would drag a wheelbarrow up the mountainside and collect coal that had fallen from the carts. This was a perk of the area, free coal to those who can carry. Another convenience not given was running water, so there were outhouses to be used and water was collected in glass jugs from a springhouse up the hillside.

While fishing and kayaking, I keep a vigilant search for Grandpa's old playground. He has told me many times of a large rock where he and his friends would meet for a swim and play king-of-the-rock for hours. I will wonder where he set his cane pole before going to eat supper and return to find a catfish, sucker, creek chub, or smallmouth bass fighting on the other end. I drift by each rock wondering where my grandfather would yell to his father to come help him cross the river to join in an early morning fishing trip before his shift.

I have asked my grandfather why he moved. He told me that he had planned on working in the mine but was not old enough. His father had passed away when he was still quite young. Grandpa took a job at a filling station in East Brady until he joined the military. When he arrived back in the States after serving a stint in Korea, he returned to a different town. The mine had closed, and the company moved on, bulldozing the houses into the dirt. It was from there that he found work in steel mills around Ohio and Western PA. He was the first in his immediate family to ever build and own his own house.

There were times we would struggle in the imagination together; my grandfather working from memory and I working from steadfast fascination. There is a road with a metal bridge that crosses Catfish Creek, and beside the road lies a much older stone bridge. The older artifact was for the railroad that is being worked on at a snail's pace to become part of the Rails to Trails movement. I have crossed both bridges on top and walked through the waters below. I look at the ancient bridge and marvel that my grandfather was able to share any stories. As a child, Grandpa and a few friends followed the tracks to the old bridge. The friends decided to walk to the river, but Grandpa decided to be a little bit sinister. He looked down from the bridge and watched butterflies flitting around a small sandbar in the creek. Still to this day he knows not what got into him but lifted a large stone above his head and set to dropping it on the colorful wings. The weight got the better of him and he lost balance, hurtling 45 feet. He tells me he would never forget the sensation of wind beating against his face for that long fall. His friends heard the plop and decided they had better check on ol' Richy and see what he'd done. They found Rich standing by a human-mold crater of sand with a large rock, inches from its head. The sand had broken his fall and his wrist.

Nothing stands in Catfish Hollow now, but Grandpa insisted the town was larger than Sarah Furnace, not that the six houses that stand in Sarah Furnace sounds large anyway. On the roadside before the bridge is a decrepit oven. Grandpa recollected plenty more and claimed they were used for baking bread. He also told me that Catfish Creek was notorious for flooding during the spring. Kinzua Dam has tamed the river since then, but the citizens of Catfish would need to be evacuated by boat during the spring. Giant chunks of ice, hundreds of yards up the mountain, were found in his youth. Now, ice hardly gains more violence than ruining some docks and raising the creek only a few feet. To think that the water level would cover a third of the mountain!

Further still down the river lies Seybertown. Our ancestors created a ferry above East Brady and the area was named after them. No records I know of exist of where the ferry was located. Grandpa shared the family history of German brothers who came here before the Revolution. Fort Seybert was in West Virginia during the 1750s, where a however-many-greats-uncle ago was commissioned by George Washington to have an area protected there for trading goods. The area was soon taken by natives who massacred 17-19 people and took another 11 captive. I will assume that the ferry business is a much calmer undertaking since there is a lack of mention in the Pennsylvania area's history.

Grandpa has pointed out a few places above the East Brady Bridge that he thinks the ferry would have crossed. Once, when I was not even a teenager, Grandpa took me out in his old white fourteen-foot boat with the outboard motor and a Northern Pike decal on the side. Hours of fishing and the only thing that either of us landed was an eight-inch smallmouth I caught that Grandpa made me feel was a trophy. The sun burned hot in the sky and no cloud appeared to give relief. "Only the greatest fishermen can catch 'em on days like this, so you know what that says about you?" he asked with a large smile and followed with his laugh. We decided that wind in our faces would be a respite from the humid heat and we cruised the deep channel. Grandpa looked at me and asked, "You ready for this?" as he let the engine idle and pointed at the steering wheel. I will never forget the sensation of the rushing wind on my face as I pushed the throttle for the first time. A loud gurgle bellowed from the stern, lapping waves spit from the bow, and Grandpa and I both nervously smiled as we violently ripped forward. He taught me how to better control the craft, taking wide, fluid turns that made me feel like we were flying. I still hear his laughs of excitement overpowering the motor as I bounced off my own waves. Even though I only captained for a few minutes, caught only one fish, and suffered itchy peeling skin from sunburn for days, no grandson could have dreamed of a better day.

There are too many of my grandfather's stories to recall. I find trying to discover the area of his youth a troubling contradiction to my natural instincts. I wish I could understand the town that shaped the man who shaped me. I can never fully understand; I must settle with the mutual love for the Alleghenies. I know when I camp near her waters, and the moon's glow illuminates the ground, I still hear the same lullaby he did. My head rests on the blue grass; I listen to the bass bellows of bullfrogs while the creeks and currents sing softly as the crickets fiddle through the night.

I have read some of the transcripts Grandpa handed to me. Each town has a lure of hidden treasure, gold coins hidden away before the

Civil War, like some local version of *The Good, the Bad, and the Ugly*. I know of no hidden treasure seekers nowadays but myself; I need no shovel to find gold.

As I revise this piece, I am haunted by something further than my grandfather's memories. I have my own son now, and on our last adventure to "Grandpa's place" we were met with new gravel driveways marked with real estate ads. Soon, the area will be littered with new camps or modern summer homes. My imagination will blur with my own memories, just as these lines blur with tears that I have lost my hero; and my son, whose namesake comes from that valley and that man, will never walk that sacred ground with Grandpa.

On Work and Being Paid

Work brought an edge to my father. He was not tall, under six feet, but he possessed solid bulk and a bearing that rough men did not challenge. I have felt that edge, recoiled from it, wondered about it often, because away from work my father was affable, gregarious, and genuine. He'd been an Infantry sergeant in the Pacific, but I sense that in war men necessarily supplant their warmer tendencies to blunt the extremes of the moment. I never knew him as a soldier, of course, but later his work presented its own extremes. Corporate competitors, weather, and a work season dwindling down to winter's crunch honed his edge. It was his way of getting things done.

I remember that edge best, even fondly now, from an exchange while we were doing a "tar-and-chip" job on a township road above the Cheat River near Point Marion. Tar-and-chip is a cheap way for local road boards to coax a couple more years of life out of a road, but motorists despise it when their tires fling tacky gravel to clatter under the fenders. Our crew had spilled several tons of clean gravel, not yet applied to the road, and my father ordered me to shovel it into a parked dump-truck. "Get that stone cleaned up," he'd roared.

Spreading the "chips" on a tar-and-chip project requires two vehicles, a truck to deliver the chips, and a hulking spreader (called a "chipper") to sprinkle them atop the asphalt goo. In flat country, the two join in mechanical coitus and trundle along, the chips sliding from the backing truck's bed continuously into the chipper's maw. But there, in hairpin curves writhing over bluffs confining the Cheat, a spill was no surprise. When the chipper turned north, the truck was still headed south.

After their spill, the "chip crew" crawled on upward, over the crest and was gone. My father went with them. I was left with my No. 4 "coal shovel," a pile of crushed stone up to my waist and instructions to move it from the ground to the empty truck. A huddle of identical shingle-sided "company houses" crowded the curve, hung on the slope for workers who built and then operated the Lake Lynn hydro-dam in the gorge below, impounding the river as the more widely known Cheat Lake. A modest porch slouched at the front of each house, and on the nearest porch, a muscular Dobermann reclined in the shade.

Each time I approached the errant pile and bent to begin shoveling, the Dobermann pricked its ears, stalked down the steps, and stood with a growl rumbling from its chest and teeth bared, inches from my offered backside. When the dog advanced, I retreated to the truck's cab. The Dobermann then returned to its station. I'd wait a few minutes, venture out, bend over to work, and the dog repeated its menace.

After several cycles of this dance, my father's pickup came rattling up around the curve (he'd gone the long way around from a turn), slinging gravel off our own finished product.

"I thought I told you to get that stone cleaned up," he snarled, slamming the truck's door.

"I tried to, but every time I start shoveling that dog comes off the porch and . . ."

"Fuck that dog! Get that stone cleaned up," was my father's barked response.

Our family had been laborers and operators of a small business in a region where work was considered its own reward. Work justified being. A "day's work" was the revered standard against which any other enterprise fell short. The worst defamation a man could suffer was to be thought a "triflin' no-account." Heroes I heard recalled as a boy were extolled for how many wagons of coal they'd shot down and loaded in a shift, for the heaped feed sacks they'd "packed" up the mountain on their shoulders, or rows of coke ovens fired and drawn. When my grandmother was extolled in posthumous conversation, it was not her teaching at one-room Hog Rocks School that was praised, but her long walk across the mountain, morning and evening, in snow, rain, and darkness. She died when I was four, and for years after her passing the only people I met who did not work with their hands and their back were my pediatrician and my priest (My mother's family was Hungarian

Catholic). Many men I knew had lost a leg, hand, arm, or eye to the mechanical violence of the ovens and mines.

Devotion to work arose in other places—the ranching West, on New England farms, in fishing communities along the coasts. But my steeping in work happened atop the bituminous coal fields of western Pennsylvania—Fayette County, which by accidents of geology, climate, and topography, giving the Monongahela River its volume to buoy barges on a northward course to Pittsburgh, plus the technology of the day—pick, shovel, dynamite, and mine pony—supplied the bulk of coal and coke that fueled Pittsburgh's rise to industrial zenith. Work here was not only important to family, it was also a cog in global metamorphosis.

Still, I never worked in a mine. My initiation to doing work came through asphalt paving—laying blacktop, spreading "tar" as you might hear it put in unpracticed vernacular. By the time I'd reached working age, which in my grandfather's and my father's shared view in the late-1960s was about 16, my family made its living laying asphalt on township roads, coal-patch alleys, parking lots, and driveways. My grandfather Curt, known by his middle name, had been a coal miner, but his open union organizing got him blacklisted by mine owners. Unable to dig coal, he started paving driveways out of a pickup truck and grew the company to modest but capable size, signing on a dozen men at a time happy to work outside the pits in open air.

My grandfather had a caustic edge at work even sharper than my father's, and it cowed me in my earliest days "on the job," which happened long before any notions of "worker sensitivity." His union tendencies prompted no deference to men in his employ. He was fair but expected work, a day's work, full-bore and efficient. Inspecting the job once, he happened along when I was wielding a hand-tamper. A hand-tamper is an eight-pound square slab of steel mounted at the end of a long hickory handle. Some person of low status is directed to slam the tamper down on wrinkles that remain in the asphalt "mat" after the mechanical roller has compacted it. The object is to tamp the still warm and malleable asphalt flat. No plan or precision is needed. Brute force and haste, before the mat cools, are the "tamper-man's" aims. Surrounded by several of my senior peers, my grandfather observed my tamping, tucked a chaw in his jaw, then remarked, "Boy, I could lay my left nut down there and you couldn't knock the juice out of it."

When other people whine about summer heat, I never speak up in agreement. An ambivalent nod is the best I'll grant them. I've helped lay tens of thousands of tons of "hot-mix blacktop" that slides out of the truck that delivered it at 300 degrees on 90-degree days. Hot weather alone doesn't wilt me. The most pointed contention between my wife and me today is that she likes to run an air conditioner in August. I'm at home in swelter.

In my early working years our equipment pool lacked late advances in paving machinery. Those coveted improvements were larger, more powerful, and versatile "pavers," self-propelled tractors that spread the mix on the road behind. Versatility came with hydraulically extendable "wings" that enabled the paver, at the press of a lever, to reach out and cover wider sections of road, extend into intersecting streets, or taper inward if a road narrowed.

The first "paver" I worked around was a rusted, tar-speckled, un-powered "drag-box," once painted yellow, and pulled along by the blacktop truck itself by wheeled arms that fit into the truck's rear wheel-well. The truck dumped a ton or two into the box, dropped its bed, then dragged the box forward to spread the mix before dumping again. Lacking its own motor, the drag-box had no hydraulics, so any widening of the road, any intersecting "apron," paved berm, or curb had to be shoveled into place "by hand." Where the box's width was too great for the road, the excess had to be shoveled up and heaped back into the box. Any blacktop left in the box at the end of a "pass" was waste unless it was shoveled back into the truck to be dumped again later. We used No. 4 coal shovels, with broad blade, short handle, and "D-grip" at the end. Smaller, ergonomic (a word we never heard) shovels were in use even then by other crews, but my grandfather had ruled them out long before, and my father continued that edict. No. 4 shovels were wide and deep, meant to move more material with each lift.

Shoveling often required you to stand atop piles of blacktop that needed moved or smoothed in-place. Blue, sulfurous vapor rose from the pile, and its heat licked up inside pant-cuffs and into rolled-up shirt-sleeves. Boot soles could melt. The upwelling heat and the sharp sulfur-smell infused every step and breath through a day. When shoveling, the tool's steel blade had a micro-cooling effect on the asphalt it carried, so that after several heavy loads, a black crust would form on the steel, increasing friction and requiring more effort to push the shovel into the pile. That crust needed frequent "cleaning," done from a 5-gallon "dip-bucket" filled with "fuel oil" (diesel) and hung on the side of the box, and later the used mechanized paver we bought at a winter equipment sale in Florida. We cleaned our shovels—every dozen or so scoops—with a long-handled brush that rode in the sloshing dip-bucket of fuel. You'd lift the oil-soaked brush out of the bucket and smear it across your shovel's face. When that oil hit the steel it crackled and sputtered against the heat, and a blue cloud of sulfur-steam bloomed up around your face. But the fuel oil cut the crust, and your next thrust into the pile of hot blacktop brought the shovel out slick, ready for more.

On one of the first days I worked, I went for my water jug, hung next to the others on hooks welded to the box, at about 9 o'clock on an already warm morning. "Best not to hit that jug too early," Chic warned, grinning around a Red Man bulge. "You won't be able to stay out of it all day, and we'll not git anything out of you."

Hand-working blacktop requires that any material shoveled into place, which does not pass under the paver's strike-off screed, must be raked by hand to match the mat, a job that called on finesse and an eye for grade. We used a "lute," a broad, flat-bladed rake on a long handle of aluminum tube made for blacktop work. The hollow aluminum shaft is light and resists overheating in the lute-man's hands. Its user bends to his work, his face meeting the heat, leveling humps and filling voids with strokes of the lute. A good luter can approximate the same smooth grade the paver would strike if it could reach all surfaces to be covered. The same crust formed on the lute blade, so the lute man carried a putty-knife in an oily hip pocket to scrape away crust, then doused his tool from the dip bucket. Most crews, ours included, have three or four shovelers to one lute-man. The shovelers get a few seconds break between heaves, but the lute-man's work is constant. The whole job's progress slows unless he keeps up, smoothing into place all the blacktop the shovelers carry to him.

I learned to lute early-on from Art, a big swarthy man with a curl of still-black hair centered on his forehead that dripped sweat onto his nose. Art could wield the lute with an ease that seemed unnatural. He was only a little younger than my grandfather, but they had known one another since they were school-skipping boys. Art taught me to lute because he seemed to believe someone named Moyer, grandson to Curt, should know how to do a skilled task. One day, at a big intersection that called for much handwork, my father complimented my skill with the lute. Such praise was not routine. It came that day out of impulse, I imagine, and everyone working nearby heard it. I can never pass that spot, even today, where Georges Township's Mud Pike intersects Rte. 857 a half-mile north of the West Virginia line, without remembering the pride that welled up inside me there.

The first job I worked on was the parking lot and connected service roads at St. Aloysius Roman Catholic Church in Dunbar (I was later married there). The parish had just built its new church on the site of the old Lazy Hour Ranch, where people had paid to take horseback rides through surrounding hills. The church lot and roads were new too, so had never been paved. We first built a base for the lot with No. 4 stone (about the size of a grapefruit but irregularly shaped), then "choked" the base by shoveling and hand-brooming fine limestone dust across the "4s" to fill the voids. The dust locked the ankle-twisting rocks into place and formed a stable platform for the asphalt to come. A day of shoveling choke-dust flocked your hair, skin, boots, and clothes white. I remember how the age-lines of older guys showed as clean brown furrows in chalk-crusted skin, tapering toward the corners of their eyes.

The next day we started paving. The cool green morning melted away under the glare of white sun, as the blacktop trucks rolled dependably onto the job. You could see them a long way off, clumps of two or three, sometimes singles, lumbering up over the rise in Ranch Road, belching smudgy exhaust. Then they made the left onto the church drive, turned around and backed up, one by one, to be hooked to the drag box.

The day was a hot one, and long before I'd acclimated to heat. One pass at a time we progressed across the lot, covering the white stone base with a two-and-a-half-inch layer of coarse blacktop. Such work grants you the benefit of seeing starkly the results of your labor—the black surface behind you is finished, the white up ahead remains undone. There is no ambiguity in such a workplace, only contrast, and a sense (exhausting at times) of progress won.

We'd dump and lay each load, and the truck, 24 tons lighter now, would seem to bounce out the driveway to Ranch Road for its return to the asphalt plant and another haul. At the start of each pass, we'd shovel in a pad of blacktop for the drag box to perch on, then the truck would dump the box full and drag it to the far end of the lot. At the end of each pass, we'd hook chains to the top of the tailgate of the truck's raised bed, so that when the driver dropped the bed, the truck lifted the box off the ground so it could be backed into place to begin the next pass. The inevitable pile of blacktop left when the truck lifted the box had to be shoveled up and heaved over the tailgate. I ran out of water by mid-afternoon, and Art sent me to a gas station to get ice for everyone's jug. When I returned, we divided the ice and filled our jugs from a garden hose behind the church. I remember how the chilled air spilled across my face when I lifted my wide-mouth jug to slurp.

Finally, we made the last pull out of the church driveway to the road. All the vast surface behind us was black, the nearest reaches still steaming where the drenching-water from the roller's steel wheels simmered away. I collapsed on the grass in the shade of a roadside tree, grateful the job was done.

But the men showed no release. They stood around oiling tools and rolling smokes. Some picked up their water jugs and began walking back across the lot toward where we'd started in the cool dawn, a lute or shovel across their shoulder. Then, a knot of three familiar trucks crested the rise, headed our way. Bewildered and dreading, I couldn't understand why my grandfather had ordered so much asphalt.

"Git up, boy. We got work to do," someone said, amused.

In the next few minutes, it became known to me that all that work of the morning and half the afternoon was to place the "binder coat," a coarse asphalt mix that serves as a base upon which the finer-grade, inch-and-a-half-thick "top" is laid as finish. By the time darkness fell at St. Aloysius, we'd covered the entire surface again, and I knew, felt in my then-supple frame, a day's work.

Our men, back then, were all older than me. They'd felled timber, loaded coal, and fought wars. They were endearingly irreverent, some ribald and others wry, at ease around merciless noise, heavy labor, heat, and (most times) each other. Their faces, hands, and forearms were brown as tobacco-spit from the sun, but dead-fish white below the V of their shirt-neck and on thinning pates under a cap. They joked about one another's relatives, their own wives, everyone's drinking, and their fading male potency. None had lived more than three miles from our shop behind my Uncle Jim's house. We knew their families and they knew ours. If I showed amusement at unsavory news about someone of common acquaintance, sun-leathered Gary would finger back his hat brim, then squint over his cigarette, hand-rolled from a Bugler pouch, to caution me: "Don't laugh too hearty. He's your relation."

The men treated me well, which meant they made me the butt of jests like everyone else, and they did not resent my close kinship to the owners. Why would they? We were working, outdoors and unfettered, on a job that was basically simple yet exacting enough to serve unspoken pride. We worked late one evening, which often happened, near to dark. The men knew I'd been seeing a girl in Dunbar, which they sometimes called "Dodge City" because of the drinking, fighting, and general carousing they knew to go on back then in the bars that lined Railroad Street. As the day waned with more trucks to dump and my amorous hopes flagging, wavy-haired, ruggedly handsome Floyd quipped knowingly, "No Dodge City for you tonight, boy." Then he'd laugh from the gut.

Working and drinking are inseparable in my memories of those men. The cool of a dark barroom, the gushy "snap" of a frosted pop-top, and that first swill of cold, malty beer, were sirens after a hot day paving. And that first swill led to so many more. Attitudes around drinking and work were different then, a credit to more responsible modern norms. But it was heady to be bought a beer in your middle teens by a man of stature who'd so signaled you a peer, with the noise, heat, and glare of the day forgotten, honky-tonk twang rising from a corner. Our whole fleet of pickups, dumps, and low-boy trailers hauling heavy equipment would wheel into some beer garden's gravel lot on the way home. The men, their clothes salt-crusted and reeking of petroleum, would settle onto stools, toss damp crumpled bills onto the bar, take a long pull, and begin telling stories about foul-ups at work, belching out guffaws between swallows. There was seldom trouble in those bars. Other patrons knew our crew were workers and respected their ease, and if they didn't respect that, we presented a formidable and unified force. Once, my father stepped into the bar, trailing everyone home as he sometimes did, had one beer, and retrieved me from the kind of fun he knew I shouldn't be enjoying at my age. But the men would stay for hours, straggling back to the shop late, then stopping their own pickups for nightcaps at Bill's Place at the foot of the mountain.

They'd report, almost unfailingly, to the shop for work at 5:30 or 6:00 a.m., depending on pre-arranged plan, feeling "rode hard and put away wet," with a quart of warm beer fisted by its neck in one brown hand. The quart was one half of their hangover cure, a remedy I have never seen, read about, or heard of, anywhere else. Once they'd settled onto the bench for the day's assignments, they'd crack open their "jumbo," and reach into a denim pocket or their dinner-bucket to retrieve an onion, big as a baseball. They'd eat that onion like an apple, yellow skin and all, then chase it down with slugs of warm beer. So fortified, they'd shake their heads, stand up, stretch, and someone would declare, "That'll straighten ya up." Ahead of them lay nine, 10, or 12 hours of continuous heavy work. Since then, especially during my days employed in government, when I've heard some people justify calling off sick, I haven't been able to accept their gazes. I could not look them in the eye without judging.

The work was seldom tedious. Most often we worked on township roads, so the jobsite was mobile, constantly moving—though slowly—through countryside and scattered communities as the trucks dumped their loads and the paver crawled along, the compacting roller bringing up the rear in its plume of steam. Except when waiting for trucks to return, which offered a welcome, uncontestable respite, we were never in the same place long, through a day or through the whole work season. We traveled all over Fayette, Greene, and Washington counties, and probed into southern Westmoreland and western Somerset when we could win bids out on our home core's perimeter. Few townships across that region had ample budgets for roadwork so, every year, they would bid to resurface the minimum that would get them by with residents rankled by the state of their roads. We'd work, maybe, three days for Stewart Township in the mountains near Ohiopyle, then load up and move west to Franklin Township for five days resurfacing narrow roads in hilly grazing land around Waynesburg. After that it could be a couple days in Point Marion, or Perryopolis, or in Redstone Township on the steep slopes above the Monongahela River outside Brownsville.

Except for the modest cities of Uniontown, Connellsville, and Washington, all our work was in rural places, and I liked that. City work, which we took when we could, was always hotter and the frequent intersections, curbs, and especially manholes demanded even more handwork. In a city with public sewers, you couldn't just pave over manholes. As the paving operation approached a manhole, its location marked by orange spray-paint on the adjoining sidewalk, the paver operator stopped and raised the screed, then moved beyond the hole while we pried off its circular lid, wrestled into place a steel "riser ring" to meet the new asphalt grade, then laid the surrounding area by hand.

Traffic added a different challenge to urban work, because our crews always lacked adequate men to both control traffic and do the work. We'd have to assign a couple laborers to "flag cars," which trimmed the number available to shovel and lute. This dilemma grew worse over time, as traffic increased, and drivers seemed to grow more intolerant of any delay.

The atmosphere was more relaxed in rural townships. Traffic was easy to manage because there wasn't much, and farm and rural working people are universally more patient with roadwork waits. Also, elected township supervisors were willing to accommodate a contractor to get the work done fast. Most would allow us to "shut 'er down." We'd put out "Road Closed" signs and orange cones, then work free of conflict. Residents along the road were allowed in and out as needed, and were unanimously happy to have us there, smoothing a road their vehicles had bucked over for years. Working in such places carried a pleasant "win-win" vibe.

Still, we had to get jobs done fast and move quickly to the next one. My grandfather, and then my father, amassed as much work as possible because you never knew how much you would win. We generally won plenty because my elders pushed the slim profit margin of public bid work to its breakpoint. Rain was a frequent impediment, though we often worked through downpours at my father's insistence. Rain before dawn could cancel work outright, but midday rain brought risk and stress (not so much to us workers), posing the choice of surrendering part of a workday versus alienating a customer by paving their road in conditions unfavorable to good results. Backlogs of unfinished contracts built tension as the days shortened and fall approached. Western Pennsylvania winters are not conducive to paving work. The material starts to "set up" even before it's dumped out of the truck. Hand-working the hardening black mass is hopeless, and it will not compact to the specified density. Our work season ended by necessity around Thanksgiving, so in October and whatever part of November the weather granted us, we worked all the daylight hours, six days every week, to complete contracts, moving around between jobs in the dark.

Paving taught me how the maze of backroads knit together across this region of hollows and knobs. If you travel only the main highways like Routes 51 and 119, or Interstates 70 or 79, your impression of the region stales, lulled by homogenous sprawl that erodes the interest of all places it taints. But we worked where you would never otherwise find your way to—Pittgas, Poland Mines, Spraggs, Nineveh, Jollytown, Upper Peanut, Lower Peanut, Chaintown, Tippecanoe, and many more, on a web of two-lane blacktop rambling and sloping through the hills. Follow any one road long enough and you're surprised where you "come out," but a map complete with contour and scale fills in inside your brain, like the way cultured microorganisms spread across a petri dish, probing, netting, connecting until they form a whole. If you placed a random pin in a map of this corner of Pennsylvania, I could describe the encompassing landscape, its shape, proportion of woodland, where its streams come from and where they're headed, and how you could get to someplace else, direct or roundabout.

I've never been sure why that feels important to me, but it does. A physical being, I find myself in a physical place. I might as well know that place, is my sense. I am from somewhere. My elders' work-edge, spurring us, grating though it could be, caused me to grasp that as deeply as I do.

I also felt pleasure in physical work. Although I sometimes chafed at the labor, its grime and long hours, its exclusion of me from the idling fun of others my age, I reveled in the corporal strain it demanded. Bending then rising, repeatedly, with a 30-pound shovel of asphalt to heave it into some bin or carrying it to sling it 10 feet to a lute man across the mat, I remember feeling a joy in (but not always) my body's capability to do that, day after day. I noted the ease of my burdened movements, lifting, pulling, hauling. When I stood aside, momentarily resting, I was easy in my stance. I was inwardly proud of the tone that rose under tanned skin, and I liked to press my nose against the muscle of my upper arm and breathe in the salt-tang. Under the shower at night, I let the salt run off my scalp and across my tongue.

I did well to sense this at the time because it will never return. The human default of youth is to not notice, to take fluidity, suppleness, and strength for granted, lost without having been internally savored, like the missed chance at a kiss you never went for, or a good stream nearby you never fished. But I did notice my strength in youth, perhaps because of the praise I'd heard heaped on ambitious miners and my teacher grandmother treading a lonely path to school.

* * *

Some years later, I looked out through a dusty window that could not be opened on the state capitol mall, lined by parallel ranks of red oaks. The oaks were my lunch-hour magnet. They drew me and I lingered under them, wondering if anyone noticed my habit. In fall, I picked up their glossy yellow-brown acorns and rolled them around in a hand, feeling their smoothness and mass.

I'd reached the window in my office through a heavy steel door to a stone-walled building that flanked the mall. The building entombed its own stale atmosphere, static and sour. Entering that air was like colliding with something beyond gaseous. It was stolid, dense with must, and unriled by current. It held a smell that never varied, a curdling sharpness. Old paper?

The office was midway down a corridor on the fourth floor. Hushed footsteps echoed along the stairways and halls. Passersby were silent, guarded. I was employed there as staffer to a committee of the State Legislature, which had been assigned a title that indicated guardianship for the state's natural resources. My title was Field Representative, a label that proved bewildering after I'd accepted the position. My "field" was the route to-and-from a parking spot behind the capitol, plus my midday flight to the oak grove. Whatever I represented was never articulated nor acclaimed.

This was not during a period of frenetic legislative action in the committee's chambers, which, in fairness, had, at times, occurred in its past. My days dragged, aimless, unchallenged, humorless. Some people can, do, master accomplishments in such a setting. I could not. I grew anxious, depressed from ennui and confinement. My body felt restless, coiled from languor. The coil unleashed in the middle of the night when I awoke in convulsion. I lashed out at my wife. I lingered in lawyer bars on the way home but found no uplift. I heard my grandfather's contempt for bureaucratic pretense that produced nothing real. Loathing for self festered.

One early fall day, an unusual thing happened. The phone on my desk rang. I answered it and a legislator assigned to the committee spoke fast, informing me that he was taking his wife to the football game at Penn State the next Saturday.

"Find me a meeting over there," he ordered.

"What kind of meeting, Mr. ——?"

"I don't care if it's some kid doing his homework. Just find me a meeting."

I made some calls to various departments whose studies bore some relevance to the committee's purview. Such a call, from an office of the State

Legislature, is accepted with eagerness by universities. Always, someone will help you find what you want. Inquiries led me to a researcher developing a mathematical model that, he envisioned, would enable vegetable growers to reduce pesticide pollution by applying minimal amounts at the optimal moment. Growers would plug the crop grown, location, temperature, precipitation, and the offending pest into his model, yielding a printout with instructions that would save a crop while cutting the use of agricultural toxins.

This researcher was incredulous that a state legislator was interested in his trials. "He wants to come here and see my work?"

"Yes," I mouthed. "The legislator wants to learn more about how it could benefit constituents." I gave him the necessary date of the meeting, on a weekend coming up quickly in September.

The man fumbled for words, clearly mulling some conflict.

"Well, my wife and I were going away on a little vacation, but I'll be available. Thank you," he said.

The legislator never showed up for the meeting. On the following Monday I had to fumble for words myself, groping to explain and apologize for one of my bosses' absence to a man who'd canceled a family trip.

If I wanted to, which I generally did not, it was not difficult to review committee-member legislators' claims for expenses. The figures and dates meant nothing to me. But at the end of that month, I did look at the expense sheets, waiting in a stack on a counter for processing. It was there, a claim signed by the legislator who'd called me, for a trip to State College, complete with receipts—mileage, lodging, and meals, justified by the meeting I had arranged. Two months later, I resigned—I already knew the difference between work and being paid.

The Year We Didn't Send Leaves

My mother was in jail
the season my son was born.
Her husband, my father, left
perplexed, shaken as the leaves

he used to mail each September.
Crispy, dried elms and oaks on fire
traversing the Ohio autumn
to North Carolina's extension of summer,

but not this equinox. This one he muttered
sounds like *visitation* and *restitution*
over phone lines that crackled
like my mother's smoker's laugh
echoing the remains of an underfoot maple.

Wilkes-Barre

Each day you buy the newspaper with pocket change, scan the classifieds in the back, circle a few to call. It takes a little while, but you catch on. Joey, a stoner metalhead kid who works in the office, too, makes it clear when you return from not viewing the third "just rented" of the day. He phones the numbers you called and they all say, *come over, still available, nice place especially for the money.* You are still young. Two years at a college that didn't fit, so back home you find a decent job for the times, which were hard all around. But it's near an hour's drive each way so you look for an apartment. Nothing much, you think, just a place to stay during the week with winter coming. Thinking it over, it is all obvious: the older woman who spoke through a cracked door, the knock that no one answered while a man sat watching in his car across the street, the woman who says her husband just called, their friend's kid is looking for a place. *Sorry about that,* she says, closes the door. Your mother always urged you to get an education: *It's something no one can ever take away from you.* That was true, regardless of what she meant. By then you'd learned some lessons. You mostly did not have to study on them too long. Your world was small, and like an Amish horse with blinders, you stared ahead, kept following a narrow road. Then you began to enter bigger worlds with harsher lessons. Standing on those porches in early November, the wind coming on, you wonder who they saw? It took years before you saw yourself: a half-breed kid born in a coal-town orphanage. It doesn't matter all that much by now. You've done well enough. You worked that job for a year, about as long as you could stand it. You tired of having your sub-shop order taken after everyone else in the place, of the clerk eyeing your license plate through the convenience store window like you were going to run off with five bucks of gas, of people asking if you worked in the store when you were wearing street clothes like them, not a blue smock and a name tag. A couple months after you left, in the worst mass murder in the state's history, a mixed-race man from that town shot and killed thirteen people including his own five children. He said he wanted to spare the kids the affliction of growing up half-caste. The sole trial defense offering was that the racism of the town had made the man insane. You wondered which slight, which slur it was that made him shake off lassitude, caused mad ire to rise and burn. When you read a newspaper account about the man and what he did you were saddened but not surprised. The weariness had begun to close upon you.

Clarity of Purpose

Slapping away flies and struggling to keep his footing on the river bottom, Joe steadied the rowboat as Martha slipped awkwardly over the side into the knee-deep water, taking care that the bundle she carried stayed dry. He caught her eye and motioned to the bank high beyond the waterline. Martha nodded and slogged the last few feet to shore as Joe hauled the boat out of the water and hurriedly concealed it among the dense brush and flood debris. Martha scrambled to higher ground and faded from sight into the undergrowth. Settling into the foliage, she turned back the corner of the bundle, exposing a tiny, silent infant. She tried to nurse the baby, but the berries, herbs, and soggy, stale corn-bread she'd eaten that morning produced no milk. The baby mouthed the nipple weakly, scrunched her face as if to cry, then fell back to sleep, exhausted by the effort.

Satisfied that the boat was out of sight and would not draw unwanted attention to his family, Joe squeezed into the thicket beside Martha. He glanced at the baby and whispered in Martha's ear. She teared up and shook her head. The couple rested until their clothes dried, then clambered up the bank and moved on. Joe carried the infant and led the way.

Days later, concealed in a thicket at the edge of a cleared Ohio homestead, they watched a farmer and his missus go about their chores while blonde, plump children played and ran about, free as yard birds. The smell of food cooking inside the house made Joe's empty stomach roll, his mouth water. Martha ignored her own hunger, but the ravages of her want were obvious in her child's listless body. The infant slept, her ragged nappy dry as a stone; her parents beyond worry that their baby would fuss and give them away.

Joe and Martha stayed put and waited out the day. They watched as the farmer put away tools, bedded livestock, and called his children inside. Dusk soon blanketed the farmstead and the small house in the clearing settled into the folds of the night. For Joe and Martha, the darkness only added to their anxiety and increased the threat that it would blossom into despair. Martha began to sob and whispered, "Maybe this ain't the right house, Joe. What if we're lost?" Joe put a finger to her lips, pulled her closer, and rubbed her back until she drifted off. When a lantern appeared in the front window of the house Joe squeezed Martha's arm, kissed the baby's head, and jumped to his feet. He darted to the door of the house and rapped lightly.

The farmer opened the door, looked nervously past Joe, and motioned him inside, his greeting a low, tense, "Hurry in, friend." But Joe stood in the doorway and turned in the direction of Martha. She rose from the security of the thicket and ran toward the house, her body bent low, the baby bundled tightly against her breasts. Joe reached out and pulled her into the house. As Martha brushed past him, he whispered, "I think we'll be safe here; he called me 'friend.'"

While the farmer secured the door, then sat the lantern on the table, his wife took in Martha's wasted frame and quickly recognized a flower going to seed. She held out her arms to take the baby and motioned for Martha and Joe to sit at the table. Within minutes the white woman had offered the limp babe a rag dipped in warm, fresh milk and ordered an older child to set out plates of food. The farmer sat down to his meal directly across the table from Joe and got serious about eating. Joe ate with quiet enthusiasm. After a few minutes of silently eating and sizing up the man at his table, the white man leaned back in his chair, cleared his throat, and stated with some authority, "I reckon it would've taken a sizable amount of gumption to make it all the way up here from where y'all started."

Without hesitation, Joe looked up from his plate and said, "It sure enough did."

The farmer sat his chair back down with a thud and smiled. "Abigale! Can you get me and this man here some more of them dumplings? I listen better on a full stomach."

The farmer, Daniel, introduced himself and began to draw Joe into a conversation. Joe spoke cautiously, questioning the wisdom of trusting a white man, even one who talked to him man to man and fed his family. But Joe's shoulder muscles loosened and his back straightened as he bore witness, his words a burden borne silently too long. Martha ate, listened, and watched with frightened, knowing eyes as her baby, too weak to suckle or cry, fell back to sleep in the white woman's arms, the rich milk of the farmer's newly freshened cow sliding down her chin, pooling in the tiny hollow of her neck.

Everyone ate their fill and the children cleared the table. The men tired of talk and the white woman passed the limp baby back to Martha, along with a sugar tit to comfort the infant. Under cover of darkness, the farmer's oldest son led Joe and Martha to the barn where they slept upon a wool blanket over clean straw, their infant between them. When morning sun filtered through the barn siding and sent straw chaff dancing upon the early autumn air, Martha rolled over and reached for her child. She found the infant dead, a tiny corncob doll, light as dried husk.

* * *

Abigale insisted upon a Christian burial. Hoping the Lord would notice her generosity, she gave Martha a faded quilt remnant from her sewing bag to shroud the dead infant. But in the privacy of the barn, Martha rocked the baby and hummed a lullaby while Joe disposed of the quilt beneath a loose floorboard. Then she tore a square of threadbare linsey from her own shift, wrapped the cold child in her own scent and warmth, and whispered to Joe, "This is so Molly'll know we're her mama and daddy when we join her on the other side."

There was little time to mourn. Martha and Joe rejoined the farmer and his family where they'd gathered in the packed dirt yard beyond their front door. Abigale wore a clean bonnet and the youngest children had clean faces and combed hair. They shuffled about and stole shy glances at the bundle in Martha's arms.

The farmer led a silent procession to his family's plot, a small clearing of graves and hand-chiseled stones in a meadow not far from the homestead. Joe supported Martha, his arm tender and protective around her shoulders as she cradled their infant. The couple remained composed, stoic in their grief in the presence of these strangers with whom they'd become so intimately, if only fleetingly, involved. Their burden eased slightly when the small cluster of tiny headstones came into view. To leave their child unattended was wrenching, but perhaps their baby would not face eternity alone.

Approaching the edge of the clearing, Abigale halted her husband. Grasping his shoulder, she attempted to turn him away from the small congregation of stones. He tried to pull free, but she stood her ground— her nails digging into his arm, her lips moving, praying silently. Daniel looked up as if God were watching and hissed, "You cannot hide your hypocrisy from God, Abigale."

"God forgive me, I will not abide my babes to make room for the infant!"

Daniel gave his wife a piercing, dark look, so chill that she took an awkward step backward and stumbled as her husband turned toward a patch of soil vaulted with brambles and blackberries at the far edge of the clearing. "Over there is good," he said in a low, husky voice. The tallest boy, carrying the shovel, nodded to his father and moved to the allotted space, but Joe, looking from father to son, held his hand out to the boy and said, "I'll take that shovel." Daniel nodded and the boy handed the shovel to Joe. Daniel and then his son took off their hats and stepped back and out of Joe's way as he began to reverently open the earth and prepare it to welcome his child. No one spoke as Joe worked; the silence was broken only by the metallic bite of the shovel entering the rocky soil, the thud of displaced dirt clods, and Joe's breathing.

Daniel stood with an uneasy readiness. His eyes darted about, and he held his gun with purpose, but he refrained from hurrying Joe. He shushed his wife with another hard look and stepped away when she sidled up to him as if to whisper in his ear. Joe took the time he needed, but no more. He stepped back from the small grave and straightened. Standing tall, he gathered to himself the calm of the quiet morning, then gently eased the baby from her mother's embrace, kissed her good night, and laid her down. Daniel mumbled a hurried *Our Father* as Joe blanketed Molly's tiny grave with dirt and leaves to foil scavengers and slave hunters. Martha sank to her knees; tearless, silent sobs racked her shoulders as she arranged three polished pebbles above her baby's head. The farmer's family averted their eyes and turned away. When Martha glanced up at Joe, he bent and helped her rise.

Daniel hurriedly repeated the directions to the next safe house, jabbing the barrel of his musket about like a compass needle pointing the way. His wife handed Martha a napkin of biscuits and cold salted pork. The two women nodded but did not speak. Abigale turned away as Martha's eyes strayed past her for a last glance at the tiny grave. The morning sun was climbing the sky and the danger of being discovered was growing. Anxious to part company, the men shook hands.

"I'm grateful for the kindness to me and my family."

"Godspeed, Joe."

Joe and Martha took their leave, the next phase of the journey no longer a vision, but a solid enterprise—mile piled upon mile, like a dry-stacked stone wall built to prevent the past from invading their future. They kept to the woods and quiet places, their slow, unthreatening pilgrimage causing little disturbance to the routine of the wildlife watching them from a distance. Joe and Martha took their cues from the animals' vigilant behavior. A bird screeching a warning call or a creature crashing through the brush and running recklessly past sent them scrambling for cover for fear that people were nearby. Throughout the day Martha's breasts began to swell, throb and leak; still, she stumbled on, her balance hindered by her arms crossed tightly over her breasts. As the shadows lengthened and the day lost its brilliance, Martha and Joe lost their clarity of purpose.

The air began to cool, thicken, and take on the grainy texture of evening. Nocturnal rustlings and utterances replaced comforting birdsong and the scolding of squirrels. Ghosts and regrets gathered in the shadows, took form, and whirled like dervishes through the congealed twilight. They grew disoriented when the clouded sky proved starless.

When Martha could go no farther, they stopped to rest. Sheltered in a remote field, lying between rows of sweetly scented, tasseled corn, they set aside the stoicism that had carried them through the day. Joe sobbed as he held Martha in his arms. The couple, having held their sorrow and the image of their baby at arms' length throughout the day, melted together, consoling one another. Only then did Martha feel the bittersweet release of her own tears and the belated letdown of breast milk. She attempted a slight smile and kissed her husband, then welcomed her baby-free rein in her heart.

Saved

At nine years old I was a sapling, all tender twigs
and folded buds. Suggestible as a bonsai,
I searched for transgressions worthy of the guilt
I felt obliged to wash away. But that day,
I surrendered, answered the call to become His—
a lamb marked with God's indelible brand.

I gripped the preacher's calloused hand and
we waded to the center of the church camp pool
where I gave myself up to him and God.
I didn't sputter or slap away his hand
when up from the watery grave I arose.

Instead, I clutched the billowy gown that floated
above my one-piece, held it down and prayed
the Clorox-flavored water had killed the germs and
inoculated the body that my Sunday school teacher
hinted would soon betray me.

The preacher lifted me upon an arc of holy spray
and deposited me onto the pool's walkway.
Words on a trajectory to God's ear: *Amen! Hallelujah!*
Praise the Lord! shot like clay pigeons from the mouths
of those gathered to witness my salvation.

The small congregation parted like the Red Sea as I
crossed the cracked concrete and ran into my father's arms.
After a squeeze, Daddy nudged me toward the crowd. His
little bee, returned to the hive—come to show the way.

I twirled politely; adults crowded around me
to memorize the coordinates of my innocence.

Overcome by the Holy Ghost or giddy with relief—
I'll never know, don't really give a damn. But it was enough,
I was a good girl with whom everyone was well pleased.
I don't recall if God was there; perhaps I'd overlooked Him
in the crowd.

Following the Pittsburgh Synagogue Massacre

I wanted to call my mother
but she is no longer there, or anywhere.

I wanted to walk Forbes Avenue
with hands in my pockets on a chilly evening,

but I am not that student anymore.
I wanted to be dropped off to art class at the museum

though its grime has been washed away;
to smell the sulfuric air on groggy summer mornings,

ride the 54C from Brentwood to Bloomfield,
pass all the neighborhoods I don't know

and wonder why I don't.
I left that city thirty years ago.

Its landscapes burned scars onto my retinas;
its people breathe in my lungs.

I left it during hard times (mine),
but now I see that troubles bind us

one by one into a new tribe
of defiance, hearts not hardened

but synchronized to bear
anything that would tear us apart.

Dead of Winter

Far from the owl's call,
from the bobcat's prints
I found next to mine,
I stare at the blue screen,
the snowy, ever-changing geography,
muttering to myself.

I'm not fooled—it's
nothing like moonlight
and makes demands of me besides.
I shut it off, which means
I am now truly alone—
you off to a meeting tonight,
last night, the night before.

I glance out the window—
a pallid, frozen sky.
The calls from a passing boom box
on the road reverberate
through the double-pane windows.
Noise travels fast in winter.

I head toward the soft comfort of quilts,
longing for the profound
stillness of the wild we left behind.
In the night, your arm slips around me.
It seems thinner than I remember
and almost weightless.
In the morning, it will disappear.

The Reading Blacksmith

Down Mansfield Avenue.
After you cross the bridge, turn right at the light.
Across the railroad tracks.
Up the street that parallels Chartiers Creek.
Third left. Sixth. Avenue, not Street.
Second block. On the right. Fourth house from the corner. 210.

I looked up at the old house for the last time. Just as well. Two of the brown Insulbrick panels up near the peak of the roof had flaked off and rested on the sidewalk. A slate shingle slid out of place and lodged in the gutter. The wooden storm windows, hung two winters ago by my father, remained mounted outside. Paint peeling. A plywood patch by the attic window still held on.

1900. The year the house was built in Carnegie, Pennsylvania, which was six years after the town was incorporated on March 1, 1894. Formed from the merger of two boroughs: Mansfield and Chartiers, once divided by Chartiers Creek. One borough had a Sixth Avenue and the other a Sixth Street.

The creek was named after the French and Native American trapper, Pierre Chartier. In 1743, he opened his trading post at the mouth of the creek. "Shirtee" was the Native American pronunciation of his name, but it was amalgamated to the more pronounced-the-way-it's-spelled "Chart-tears." The creek runs for 52.4 miles until it joins the Ohio River at a point three miles downstream from Pittsburgh. The same way our glass pop bottles plugged with river mud floated if we couldn't sink them with our BB guns.

The town was named after Andrew Carnegie, who was so honored by the request to be the namesake for the newly formed borough that he donated one of his libraries to the town in appreciation. (It opened May 1, 1901, with the official name: Andrew Carnegie Free Library. Of the

2,509 libraries built by Andrew Carnegie, it was the only public library granted permission to use both his first and last names. That same year, Andrew Carnegie sold the Carnegie Steel company and earned $226 million.)

1960. The year my father bought the house. He would die there 46 years later.

2008. The house had sold, two years after my father's death, and my hold on it, as the executor for my father's estate, would dissolve at the closing. I was there to remove the few things I had held back from the estate sale and locked in the cellar way. Unable to keep them, unable to give them up, I had waited to return until the last possible day.

So one last time. (Of course, sometimes what becomes the last time isn't by our own design or choosing, nor do we realize at the time that it is to be the last.) Up the three stone slab steps to the concrete walk that curved around to the back door. Past Mr. Coleman's porch. The houses were built close together. A hedge, a walkway down the center, and a squared-off forsythia bush were all that would fit in-between. I still thought of that house next door as Mr. Coleman's even though he had passed away while I was in college and two other families had lived there since.

F. Leo Coleman, the President of Carnegie Savings and Loan, and our next-door neighbor for many years, granted the mortgage for our house to my father. In the summer, Mr. Coleman sat on the porch every evening smoking a cigar and listening to the radio broadcast of the Pirates' baseball games. He kept an autographed baseball from the 1960 World Series winning Pittsburgh Pirate team in his Savings and Loan office.

All through the baseball season, cigar smoke and radio chatter would blow back through the screens of our house. Only the whistle and rumble of the freight trains would drown out Bob "The Gunner" Prince's call of the game.

My father detested both smoking and baseball.

Boxing. That was my father's sport.

I walked to the back porch and the kitchen door. The front door was for guests. Friends and family always knocked at the back. I looked at the stone walls that held back the hillside that our yard was carved from and the back of the duplex that stood on the leveled plot above. Our house rested on the sheet cake pan while the duplex behind us rested on the cake.

A quick glance at our backyard. The grass no longer flattened but overgrown.

When I was a child, we didn't have many books in our house. A Bible, of course. A red Thorndike-Barnhart dictionary, created in the twentieth century to be a "school-aged" readers' dictionary by the educational psychologist, Edward Thorndike and his lexicographer and editor, Clarence Lewis Barnhart. And a set of World Book Encyclopedias, the 1960 edition, 20 volumes.

That's what I was here to collect.

I opened the cellar way door. Covered with thick oil-based mahogany paint except the lower corner where the paint had been clawed away by our cat, Sparky, when he got locked in the cellar.

I dragged the white, wood-grained, composite bookshelf, custom-designed by the encyclopedia company and offered as a customer incentive to hold the encyclopedia set, into the empty living room. The shelf could only hold 17 of the volumes. The T, U-V, and W-X-Y-Z volumes lay on top of the rest of the set along with the dictionary and Bible. My hand pressed down on the Bible and dictionary that rested on top of the loose encyclopedia volumes as I dragged them into what was once our living room.

From the floor (I remembered sitting on the same blank floor when we moved in but with wooden blocks stacked beside me instead of books. I was three. My sister, a newborn), I opened the red cloth cover of the dictionary. A red dot by each word my dad and I had studied together. The dots stopped at the Ls. I set it aside.

The Bible had been held together with a rubber band around the cracked black pebbled-leather cover. The gold flaked off the embossed lettering on the cover, "Holy Bible" still discernable. An impression on the black pebbled-leather cover. An inverse Braille.

The rubber band broke as I removed it from the old King James Version Bible and turned to 1 Corinthians 13:4-8. The page had come loose from the binding. (That same verse was inscribed on a plate my father hung on the kitchen cabinet for a time until it was bumped from its hook and shattered on the floor.)

I started to read the verse aloud but finished silently as I noticed the verse bracketed by my father's handwritten note.

> [4] Charity suffereth long, and is kind; charity envieth not; charity vaunteth not itself, is not puffed up,
> [5] Doth not behave itself unseemly, seeketh not her own, is not easily provoked, thinketh no evil;
> [6] Rejoiceth not in iniquity, but rejoiceth in the truth;
> [7] Beareth all things, believeth all things, hopeth all things, endureth all things.
> [8] Charity never faileth: but whether there be prophecies, they shall fail; whether there be tongues, they shall cease; whether there be knowledge, it shall vanish away.

Carefully turned through the pages.

Found his handwritten notes throughout the margins of the Bible. At the point of each curvy bracket, "Read to Ken" and the date. The brackets flowed around all 1,189 chapters. The dates all within the first four years of my life. Many pages now unattached from the binding.

The encyclopedia volumes were stuffed alphabetically with ticket stubs, newspaper clippings, and old elementary school assignments.

I opened the "B" volume to "Boxing." A *Pittsburgh Press* clipping describing Sugar Ray Robinson's boxing match with Joey Archer on November 10, 1965, at the Civic Arena in Pittsburgh. Dad's cursive "Ken and I were there," in the left-hand corner of the picture from the article.

Leading up to the fight, Sugar Ray Robinson had been training at a gym on the Northside. Dad took me. I can't remember much anymore. Not the name of the gym or the street. Just how we crossed an old plywood plank over a mud puddle where the sidewalk was missing on the path to the gym. Inside, sweat, canvas, leather and rosin mingled into a single scent. Dad led me up close and I stood just outside the arc of the leather rope. TapTapTapTap. There he was, Sugar Ray Robinson, former Middleweight Champion, "Pound for Pound," the greatest boxer in history. He skipped rope as his trainer whistled "Sweet Georgia Brown." I watched Dad's hand rested on my shoulder. I was almost eight.

The fight. Our seats were in the last row at the top of the Civic Arena. The fight lasted the full ten rounds. Everyone who knew anything about boxing expected the outcome. I held out hope as the two fighters joined hands with the referee in the center of the ring. Waiting. A quiet rumble. A train approaching from far away. The vibration like standing on the track. "Ladies and Gentlemen." ClangClangClang. Like a railroad crossing warning. The bell of the timekeeper at ringside. Nine thousand and twenty-three people waited. "Your attention please." The train rushing closer. Louder. Pounding the ground. Pushing the air.

"And the winner by unanimous decision." The referee raised Archer's hand. The sound blaring. "Joey Archer." Roaring. Then it was past. A distant rumble fading. (It would be Sugar Ray Robinson's last fight. His boxing career, over.) But the sound blasted through again. Cheering. Dad was Cheering. Why? Sugar Ray lost. We wanted him to win. He had shaken my hand that day at the gym. It was too loud for Dad to hear my question. He couldn't feel my tug on his pant leg. We left the arena. (Much later I came to realize what the cheering was about.)

I returned the encyclopedia volume back to the shelf. It barely fit. Tight with all the stuffing.

That was it. Twenty-two books. The last things to leave the old house.

I remembered my father's old joke: Books? We have more. Five million, two hundred thirty thousand, and two hundred. And one. To be exact. They're at the library. (Not our small-town library, but an even more famous one.)

And we went there almost every Sunday. The Carnegie Free Library of Allegheny in the Northside neighborhood of Pittsburgh. The building was commissioned in 1886. Grant amount $481,012.00. Designed by John L. Smithmeyer and Paul J. Pelz in their Romanesque revival style. (The pair had also designed the Library of Congress building in 1883.) This was the first Carnegie Library to be commissioned in the United States. It was dedicated by Andrew Carnegie and President Benjamin Harrison on February 20, 1890.

It was like our church. Magnificent. Roman and Byzantine. A stronghold. Massive granite bricks. Rough-edged. The overall surface like ruffled feathers rendered in stone. The square clock tower with its pyramid roof rose twice as high as the rest of the building. It shadowed the stone-arched entrance like a sentry.

Inside white marble floors. Slippery and cool to the touch. The slap of my leather-soled Buster Brown shoes whapped in the atrium just before the inner door. The reading room entrance triple-arched like a Greek temple lit by skylights in the vaulted ceiling. Heavy, dark brown oak shelves solid enough to stand on. And you had to be quiet. Just like church. Only hushed whispers. Often my father's index finger pressed against his lips as he faced me.

Our first stop. The card catalog. It seemed football-field long. My father searched the narrow drawers for a book he wanted me to get. Wrote down the Dewey Decimal System numbers for the book on a slip of paper. Just the numbers. Like a combination to a lock. 832.8. He waited there as I went to look. A code and a scavenger hunt, all in one. I found it. *The Jungle Book*. The book he thought best for me to practice my writing. Cursive. I was in third grade.

I went to the children's section and scooted my chair, with a squeak, up to the table. I took out my Harding Elementary School templates, the pages filled with three lined rows. Two bold with a dotted line through the center, so you'd know where to stop at the top of the small "a" and where the bottom of the "b" should start. During that year, I copied stories, longhand, from *The Jungle Book* on those lined pages.

This one I found still tucked in the encyclopedia under K:

Nag slipped through the drain into the bathroom. His head came first, then his five feet of scaly body. Rikki-tikki was angry, but also afraid. He stayed very still for an hour. Then, he moved slowly toward Nag. He knew he had to kill Nag with his first bite. Rikki jumped on Nag's head. Nag shook him every which way. Though Rikki was dizzy and hurt all over, he held on tightly.

The stories were the best part of practicing my Palmer Method penmanship. After the third grade, as the second-place cursive writing winner, my father brought me back for the stories.

From the third grade through the eighth, we seldom missed a Sunday. I checked out a book a week, sometimes more. I loved how the librarian wrote my name on the borrower section of the card tucked in the pocket of the inside front cover. I loved being on that list with all the readers that had come before me.

With my books under my arm, we always walked past the statue.

"The Reading Blacksmith." That sculpture was part of the monument to Pittsburgh industrialist Colonel James Anderson. Colonel Anderson served under General William Henry Harrison in the War of 1812 and in 1827 he built the first iron mill in what would later become Pittsburgh. He was considered a pioneer in the manufacture of iron.

The monument was a gift from Andrew Carnegie and was placed just outside the library.

A bust of Colonel Anderson on a polished granite wall topped the monument. Near the bottom, a bronze plaque read:

"To Colonel James Anderson, founder of free libraries in Western Pennsylvania. He opened his library to working boys and on Saturday afternoon acted as librarian, thus dedicating not only his books, but himself to the noble work. The monument is erected in grateful remembrance by Andrew Carnegie, one of the "working boys" to whom were thus opened the precious treasures of knowledge and imagination through which youth may ascend."

Upon the block of granite that holds the plaque sits the bronze statue of "The Reading Blacksmith." It was sculpted by Daniel Chester French, the sculptor of the statue of Abraham Lincoln enshrined in the Lincoln Memorial in Washington D.C.

The sculpture is of a slightly larger-than-life laborer. The man sits on an anvil wearing a hat, its brim rolled up in place; his shirt is removed and rests draped on his right, and he wears dungarees with rolled-up cuffs that just touch the tops of his work boots. A sledgehammer rests against the anvil on his left. A book is open on the figure's lap, as he hunches over the book and his right hand grasps the pages at the top.

A lot of that is gone now.

Andrew Carnegie died from bronchial pneumonia at his Shadow Brook estate in Lenox, Massachusetts, on August 11, 1919. (Andrew Carnegie wrote, "The man who dies rich dies disgraced," in his June 1889 essay, "Wealth." Prior to his death at age 83, he had given away $350,695,653. After his death, his last $30,000,000 was given to foundations, charities, and to pensioners.)

The books from his library are still there. Nearby. In a new building. A pale grey, smooth-walled, low-slung modern design. Named the Allegheny Branch of the Carnegie Library of Pittsburgh (CLP.)

The building I visited so many times with my father is no longer a library. In 2006, a lightning strike to the top of the clock tower blasted its spherical granite finial down through the roof like a cannonball. It rattled into that building like a shotgun pellet through the skull. And weakened the structure like cancer to a body. The resulting damage caused the library to close.

On April 19th, that same year, my father died, by his own hand, in our backyard.

* * *

2018. I chose a fall day. First Resurrection Cemetery, then Allegheny Commons Park. Grey drizzled wet leaves were everywhere. I returned to the old library, now surrounded by chain link fence and construction notices. *Keep Out. Authorized Personnel Only.* Padlocks and chains. A mote of mud. What grass was left had been flattened. The windows boarded. Or blackened. Or flapped with plastic sheets. Shut off. Blind. But high up the clock tower still rose. The big gold Roman numerals were faded, but the hands of the clock had been brightened. The big hand moved over another minute as I watched. The big stone building crouched but held on.

At least one thing seemed the same from our visits.

The Reading Blacksmith was still across from what had been the main entrance. The bronze colored and streaked by the weather. (Metallurgists say steel is stronger than bronze. But steel will rust. Time and weather will weaken it. But bronze—bronze protects itself from those two. Stronger in their presence. In the weather, bronze oxidizes superficially. Its copper oxide coating hardens. Becomes copper carbonite. The underlying metal protected from corrosion.)

The semicircle granite benches that curved out around him from each side were empty. Alone. But he sits on his anvil. Bent over the book in his lap. Hat on. His shirt tossed at his feet. He still holds his book, but the handle is missing from his hammer. Only the sculptor's indentation for its resting place left in the anvil that was the blacksmith's seat. Things fall apart at the end. Pieces missing. Worn out. Nothing lasts.

But something remains.

Prospice

(Written by Robert Browning in the autumn of 1861 months after the death of his wife. Published June of 1864 in the "Atlantic Monthly.")

Fear death? —To feel the fog in my throat,
The mist in my face,
When the snows begin, and the blasts denote
I am nearing the place,
The power of the night, the press of the storm,
The post of the foe;
Where he stands, the Arch Fear in a visible form,
Yet the strong man must go:
For the journey is done and the summit attained,
And the barriers fall,
Though a battle's to fight ere the guerdon be gained,
The reward of it all.
I was ever a fighter, so—one fight more,
The best and the last!
I would hate that death bandaged my eyes and forbore,
And bade me creep past.
No! let me taste the whole of it, fare like my peers
The heroes of old,

Bear the brunt, in a minute pay glad life's arrears
Of pain, darkness and cold.
For sudden the worst turns the best to the brave,
The black minute's at end,
And the elements' rage, the fiend-voices that rave,
Shall dwindle, shall blend,
Shall change, shall become first a peace out of pain,
Then a light, then thy breast,
O thou soul of my soul! I shall clasp thee again,
And with God be the rest!

—Robert Browning

I kept the Bible. My sister has the dictionary. The encyclopedias and all their contents were sent to recycling.

The author would like to thank Professor William Lychak of the University of Pittsburgh for his instruction, advice, and encouragement in the art of writing.

Illuminated

The night of the closest supermoon
in 70 years, I scrolled through

Facebook posts of my friends' photos.
Peter's was best: the moon floated

like an illuminated balloon above a red barn
in Roaring Spring. I'm ashamed

to say how long it took me to look
outside at the real thing.

Iris

Delirium—
an iris sipping
sunset
till its beard
dribbles
dusk.

Snarl

An icy snarl
down
by the creek—
how long
till the river
misses
its teeth?

First Principles

"It's not worth it," I muttered, fighting the urge to grab a handful of Ellen Winthrop's cultivated curls and give a yank. As part of the mob erupting from Walker Elementary, she had shoved her way past Bobby and me, sending an elbow into my ribs as good measure. The mayor's pampered daughter was a prime example of a fact I'd learned to live with: The small river town of Walker, Ohio, bred an elitist class of scholars whose pedigree carried more weight than academic prowess or common courtesy. Good sense had also kept me out of trouble the day Ellen took one look at Millie Wallace's maxi-dress and trumpeted: "My mother gave that to Goodwill!"

Millie was what they called "slow" before everybody threw around terms like "learning disabled" and "developmentally handicapped." But she knew an insult when she heard one, and her face glowed as red as her hair. On a good day, Millie's life was no walk in the park. Her father couldn't hold his liquor and her older twin brothers prowled around Walker like a pair of renegade wolves, so a nice dress should have been a treat. I'd been all set to tie into Ellen until the look on Millie's face told me the last thing she needed was prolonged attention. Instead, I disassociated myself from the fringes of Ellen's elite cadre, and in return she'd never forgiven me.

* * *

By the time I reached the fan-cooled kitchen at home, I'd dismissed Ellen's jab as inconsequential. Eager to meet Bobby for our great adventure, I packed PB&J sandwiches on white bread and Oreo cookies while Mom reeled off her list of precautions—watch out for snakes, poison ivy, and strangers. She concluded with, "Be home before dark." Rarely, if ever, did Bobby mention his mother's restrictions. Without a man in the house, his mother pulled as many hours as she could at Banger's, Walker's lone watering hole, and seldom got off before two a.m. Of course, the finer folks of Walker cast a cloud of disapproval over Bobby, his older brother Sam, and the woman who supported them. Sensitive to a fault and too proud to accept charity, Bobby had insisted on picking up chips and sodas at the gas station on his way to our meeting place.

For weeks, we had been planning to celebrate the end of sixth grade by hiking the overgrown foot-trail that wound throughout a spot of woodland adjoining Walker and ending, along with Mill Creek, at the Muskingum River. By the time we met up where Mill Creek Road dead-ended and the longest section of the trail began, the afternoon had turned hot and muggy, and I wondered why Bobby wore long sleeves and jeans. But entering the overgrown path, I envied his forethought and regretted my choice of shorts and sleeveless blouse. Nettles stung my legs and strands of multiflora rose tore viciously at my hair and arms. Using Bobby's penknife, we made walking sticks out of fallen branches to fight our way through the wilderness.

Eventually, we entered a pine copse where the forest floor changed from packed-down leafy mulch to a bed of fallen needles, some kicked about as though recently trampled. Silence among the pines was intense, and nothing stirred, not even the air. A few feet ahead, something shiny caught a beam of sunlight through the branches. Bobby picked up a keyring from which a fob and two Ford keys dangled. He glanced at the inscription, and without offering to share his find, stuck it in his pocket. My curiosity soared, but I knew that Bobby never opened up about things until he was ready, and pestering just delayed the process.

Not long after we cleared the pines, we spotted the narrow creek bordered by mossy rocks. We dipped our hands into the cold stream and splashed water on our faces. Bobby's stomach growled, reminding me that I was hungry too, so we spread our provisions on a flat rock and polished everything off, wordless the entire time. Bobby's wide gray eyes revealed deep thinking, making me even more curious about the key chain. It was all I could do to keep my mouth shut.

We put bottles and wrappers in his backpack and picked up the trail again. Ahead, a break in the undergrowth marked an intersecting trail, a shorter route back to Walker, but we had agreed upon the long haul. We passed the corner formed by the adjoining footpaths where a sandstone foundation and rotting timbers were evidence of someone's home. Whoever had lived there had enjoyed flowers: overgrown lilac bushes bore the remains of fragrant purple blossoms, and a row of dark green peonies budded with promise after all those years.

When Bobby and I met the creek again, its waters were tumbling over a rocky ledge, creating a rainbow and forming a pool. Water spiders danced on the quiet surface, and our sudden presence startled a deer catching a drink. We watched its graceful retreat and the white tail disappearing into the trees like an afterthought.

* * *

What seemed like a long time later, the hum of tires on metal grating and a glimpse of arching bridge supports through the treetops signaled that the trail, along with the creek, was about to end. Soon, from a sandy shoreline, Bobby and I would see the Muskingum running its peaceful course south, its waters as smooth as glass. Then, just ahead, the river would meet a sudden concrete drop and become a roiling and frothing maelstrom. The continuous roar of the dam was as familiar and reassuring as my own breathing.

Underneath these welcoming sounds I detected something that didn't belong and stopped to listen, pulling on the back of Bobby's shirt. Someone was sobbing, painfully and desperately, and choking for gasps of air. In less than a second, Bobby had shoved me to the ground, dropped to his belly, and begun inching closer to the source. Straining my neck, I observed Bobby's head drop to the ground and his shoulders convulse as if a weight had dropped on him. Then he inched back to my side where he lay motionless and silent, his face buried in his arms. The sobbing I'd heard was replaced by the sound of footsteps stumbling across stones and exposed tree roots and then gradually fading away. Finally, all I could hear were tires crossing the bridge, waters tumbling over the dam, and the usual rustlings and chirpings of the woods. Bobby still hadn't moved. I nudged him once, then again, harder. He lifted a face covered in tears and dirt. "It was my brother," he said. "I think Sam killed Johnny."

I scrambled to my feet and crept toward the trampled ground on both sides of the creek. Bobby was suddenly beside me, and together we stood over Johnny Winthrop, the mayor's son, lying face-down in the creek, his head bearing evidence of a hideous crushing blow. A trace of reddish creek water eased around the dampened plaid bell bottoms and the soles of platform shoes before bleeding into the Muskingum where it dispersed. The tableau before us was beyond belief. My brain's inability to grasp its reality provided the emotional distance I needed to hold myself together and make a reasonable statement: "We have to tell somebody."

"Don't even say that!" Bobby grabbed my arms and shook me so hard I heard my teeth rattle. Bobby's reaction scared me more than the grizzly sight. I tore myself free and made a panic-driven dive for the narrow, treeless shoreline. Bobby tried to grab me, but I was too quick for him and pelted along the strip of sand, river to my left and woods to my right. Sensing he was gaining on me, I stared ahead, knowing if I looked back it would cost me whatever lead I had. It was his panting and sobbing that eventually brought me to my senses and my flight to an end. Bent at the waist, I waited for him to catch up, and we both dropped to the ground. Even as Bobby's breathing eased, tears continued to track down his face.

"You said they were friends, Bobby. You don't think...."

He cut me off, his voice hoarse and raw as if the words hurt coming out. "There's more to it than that."

Right then, I wasn't sure I'd comprehend an explanation if Bobby gave one. He stood and pulled me to my feet. "We have to stay quiet about this. Do you hear me? Stay quiet until I can talk to Sam."

My head nodded in agreement and my feet moved toward the bridge where an occasional car and pickup crossed. If people looked down, they could see two kids on the path at the river's edge appearing dazed and staggering like drunks. I had to pull myself together, and I sensed Bobby making the same effort. When we reached Bridge Street, the sun had slipped below the hills and its afterglow was tinged with evening pink just like the creek water I'd seen flowing into the Muskingum. The image of a bloody trickle giving way to the river current seemed like something from a dream. As we parted ways, I said, "Let me know," in a voice I didn't recognize as mine.

* * *

Supper dishes were piled in the sink, and my parents lingered over their coffee cups, neither in a hurry to stir. The sleeves of Daddy's work shirt were rolled past the elbow and his muscular forearms rested easily on the checkered oilcloth. Traces of dust from handling bags of grain at the feed mill clung to his hair and eyebrows. Mom's expression noted my presence and Daddy turned. "How was your hike, Punkin'?"

I answered, "Fine." A pitcher of tea drew my attention, and I took a glass from the cupboard and willed my hand steady enough to pour it.

"If you're hungry, there's stew on the stove," Mom offered.

"No thanks, I'm going upstairs."

Something in my demeanor caused her sixth sense to kick in. "You look flushed. Come over here." The hand on my forehead was cool and firm, as quick to spot irregularity as was its owner, but I made it out of the kitchen without a grilling.

I hadn't expected to sleep a wink that night, but by the time I had bathed, donned a nightshirt, and tumbled into bed, my body and brain had worn themselves out, and I was dead to the world the minute my head hit the pillow. Sometime during the night, the sound of pebbles against glass awakened me. The last time pebbles had been tossed at my window, my dad's feet had hit the floor and Bobby got an earful about sneaking around at night and disturbing people's sleep.

"Johnny's body is gone," Bobby rasped out the minute I appeared at the window.

Even from my perch, I felt his desperation. "Gone?"

"Yes, gone. Come on. I'll show you."

"My dad would kill me. What did Sam have to say?"

"He never came home."

"Maybe he's there now. Go on home, Bobby. Please, don't get yourself into trouble."

Bobby looked like he had more to tell me, but something changed his mind and he turned and headed up the street. One minute, every detail of his dragging walk and drooping shoulders was as sharp as day in the moonlight. The next, shadows swallowed any trace of him. As I turned back to my warm nest, a chill went down my spine. We could both be in trouble already. We'd seen a dead body and hadn't told a soul. Worse, we may have seen the killer. Even under the covers, I shivered from a feeling worse than cold.

* * *

"Johnny Winthrop is missing," Mom informed me first thing the next morning. Her day always began with a cup of strong black coffee and the morning news via a turquoise transistor on top of the fridge. My legs suddenly felt weak, and I sat down hard at the table. Since the words "Johnny's gone" had been running through my head like an eight-track loop since dawn, it was a wonder I didn't respond with "I know."

The newscast included a plea from Mayor Winthrop himself: "Anyone who has seen my son John Junior since yesterday morning or who knows anything of his whereabouts, call immediately." The mayor's private number followed. Then a DJ brought up the opening bars of "I'll Be There," and the bell-like voice of a young Michael Jackson flooded the kitchen.

If my daily routine wavered one iota, Mom would begin piecing together her impressions from last night with minute bits of evidence I hadn't known I'd dropped. So even though the last thing I felt like was eating, I shook cereal into a bowl and poured on milk as I did every morning. I forced myself to swallow bite after bite of half-chewed Cheerios while I tried to figure a way to hail Bobby without her knowing. Then the wall-phone rang, a stroke of luck I couldn't have planned better myself, and I leaped for it.

* * *

The smell of wood polish and antiquity met Bobby and me as we entered the library that morning. The librarian, faded and fragile, smiled. She invariably carried two pencils, one over each ear, but she could never find one when she needed it. I always touched my ear as a wordless reminder, making me one of her favorites. Bobby and I pretended to browse, took two random titles off the shelves, and found a secluded corner. I led off with something that had been troubling me since yesterday: "What did you mean by 'more to it than that' when I asked you about Johnny being Sam's friend?"

Bobby had already told me Sam hadn't been home yet. When I'd asked if *he'd* gone to bed at all last night, he'd just shrugged. Now, he gave me one of those looks that tested the validity of my question. "So you don't know?"

"Would I ask if I did?"

He sighed and held out his hand, palm down, and tipped it side to side.

"Oh," I said.

There were plenty of folks around town who suspected the mayor's privileged son, snotty Ellen Winthrop's brother, preferred guys over girls, and in a place like Walker, Johnny's flashy wardrobe lent credence to the rumor. But when it came to Sam, I would never have guessed. His eyes were wide and dreamy like Bobby's but brilliant blue instead of somber gray. His hair was a streaky blond, cut in a 70s shag, while Bobby's sandy thatch tumbled whichever way it pleased with no attempt at style. Every time Sam saw me, he said, "Hey, Doll Face, what's happenin'?" I knew he was just being nice to his little brother's friend, but that didn't keep my face from flushing or my pulse from pounding. Bobby's revelation made me reconsider my painful crush on his brother Sam, but that was nothing compared to what Sam, Bobby, and their mother would face if word got out.

Bobby finally told me what he hadn't done last night. When he had stopped to buy chips and pop for the hike, the Wallace boys were fueling their rust bucket pickup. One of them mentioned Johnny Winthrop and the other said, "Shut up fool." No one paused for long when passing by a Wallace, so that's all Bobby heard.

He fished the keyring out of his backpack and laid it on the table. "I knew when we found this that Johnny had been on the trail. I never expected to find him dead. Or my brother standing over him like he'd done something terrible, freaking out."

I remembered the disturbed bed of needles just inside the pine copse and picked up the keyring from the table to read the inscription on the fob: "John David Winthrop, Junior." Switch key and door key jangled slightly as I slid them into my pocket. An early graduation gift, Johnny's new red Thunderbird had made a lot of eyes pop around town; most first vehicles were family hand-me-downs or hot rods kids fixed up themselves. Bobby yawned and laid his head on the library table. Despite the gravity of the situation, he would have been asleep in seconds if I hadn't shaken his arm. "There's nothing you can do until you talk to Sam. Go home and get some sleep."

Outside, the day was heating up, but when we parted company at Bridge Street, storm clouds were massing on the western horizon. Rain came early in the afternoon and ended in a sun-shower with a rainbow stretching from hilltop to hilltop, countless times larger than the mini-bow formed by the waterfall in Mill Creek.

Bobby's second call of the day came later that afternoon, and from the squeak, as Bobby closed the door, I knew he was in one of the two phone booths in Walker. "Sam came home," he blurted, his words drowning my quick "Hello?"

"Good," I said. "Now, we can all go to the police chief and explain everything."

"Not so fast," Bobby countered. "He was worn out and starving and almost asleep on the couch when I went to the kitchen to make him a sandwich." He paused to take a breath. "Next thing I knew, the Wallace brothers were kicking in the front door and grabbing Sam off the couch. I should have done something, but I just stood there in the kitchen like a dope!" Bobby choked on a sob but found his voice: "They said something about an insurance policy and dragged him out to their pickup."

"But you did call the cops, right?"

Anger sharpened Bobby's speech: "Who do you think would talk to me? A boater spotted what they think is Johnny's body in the river and everybody's at the marina waiting for the rescue team. That includes the constable and the sheriff and both deputies. Come see for yourself. Just try to get somebody to listen. But if you really want to help Sam, meet me behind Benning's Hardware."

Bobby hung up before I could get another word out. Since Dad was at work and Mom was grocery shopping, I stuck a note on the fridge saying I was with Bobby and took off.

* * *

From the top of the rise on Halcyon Street, just across from the hardware, I could see what Bobby was talking about. Two sheriff's cars were nosed into the graveled parking lot beside the marina. A truck with Army Corps of Engineers printed on the cab doors was backing a boat trailer down the ramp. A couple of men in khaki got out of the cab, spent a few minutes talking to the sheriff, and then launched a gunmetal gray rescue boat. They jumped aboard, powered the engine, and began a measured, methodic cruise downriver in the wake of a red fishing vessel. Other boats, freed from their moorings and idling, kept their distance.

Onlookers continued to assemble as Mayor Winthrop and the sheriff stood on the bank; a sheriff's deputy and Walker's rotund constable enforced an invisible boundary around the officials. From where I stood, it appeared that the mayor's attention never left the rescue boat once its grappling hooks dropped, and their chains rattled ominously against the hull.

I was so locked into the scene that I jumped when Bobby grabbed my arm. He led me to the secondary trailhead behind the hardware store. A block up from the store the Wallace twins' pickup sat as though ready for a quick get-away. It appeared that Bobby's thinking had been right on. It was something the Wallace twins would do—take Sam to where Johnny had died. What they had planned for Sam was anybody's guess, but it couldn't be good.

At that point, I shook myself free from Bobby's grip and stood my ground. "No matter what you think, Bobby, it's time to tell the police."

"Call the cops, call the cops! Can't you get off that kick?" Bobby shook the fall of sandy hair forcefully from his forehead probably the way he'd like to shake me. "What are you going to say? That we found Johnny's dead body yesterday? That my brother Sam was standing over him?"

"But what can we do by ourselves?" I tried to keep the frustration out of my voice but failed miserably. "We're only a couple of kids!"

"We can see what's happening to Sam, that's what." Bobby's eyes, usually reflecting far-reaching thoughts, were focused on the job at hand and hard as slate.

Instead of responding, I studied the trailhead. Camouflaged by domestic hedge, the entry showed signs of recent disturbance and struggle where feet bearing distinct types of footwear had scuffled in the rain-softened ground. I stepped farther in, where heel marks of sneakers indicated the wearer had been dragged; tracks of the work-boot wearers who had dragged him showed up on either side. Bobby's urgency made him careless as he charged ahead. Prompted by an instinct I must have picked up from Mom, I pushed him away from the tracks. I also slowed his headlong rush by grabbing his wrist and making him face me.

"Okay, Bobby. I'll go along with this, but here are the rules. We stay out of sight. We don't make a sound. And we don't do anything stupid."

Bobby nodded; I stepped aside and let him lead the way. Together, we crept silently beside the tangle of boot tracks and the pair of heel tracks until we reached the fork. The fading scent of lilacs had been a pleasant surprise yesterday and had set my imagination reconstructing life in a snug little house in the woods. Today, my senses were solely tuned to ensuring our silence and survival. Had my foot broken a twig, had our passing disturbed the underbrush and startled birds into sudden flight? Did a freshet from the day's rain mask noises I should be hearing? Was the rustle of leaves high in the branches or closer to the ground?

As we neared our destination, my stomach grew queasy. Fearsome scenarios teased their way into my thoughts. It was time to take stock. Bobby's expression reinforced my evaluation, and we stood absolutely still, our full attention on the sounds of the forest and what had become by that time a steady hum of tires crossing the bridge. I was first to hear the barest of aural signals that didn't belong here: voices, maybe fists on flesh, the disturbance of verdant undergrowth. The specification of voices and words grew more and more distinct as we crept silently forward. My mouth against his ear, I whispered. "Don't even think about going in there, Bobby."

If he heard me, the words didn't register. I sensed his muscles, fists, and teeth clenching. He jumped to his feet and before I could grab him, he was running toward the melee, mindful of nothing—a reasonable course of action, caution, or even the certainty of danger. My dad always said that one fool was one too many, so I dropped to the ground as quietly as I could and edged toward the sounds bit by bit, checking each movement for anything that could give me away. When I dared go no farther, I sheltered among outsized clumps of broadleaf dock, pretending silence would make me invisible. I had a momentary flash of a game my parents used to play with me. I'd cover my head with a blanket, and they would pretend they couldn't see me. They let me think my giggles gave me away.

"Well, look at this! Come to save your big brother, little feller?"

The voice was nearby. I tried to imagine myself as small as the guy in *The Incredible Shrinking Man*, a movie I'd watched on late night TV with the sound turned so low it wouldn't wake my parents and get me in trouble.

I heard sudden movement: someone grabbed Bobby. More movement: he was on the ground.

A voice, maybe Sam's, strained to be heard through binding. Then one of the Wallace boys spoke to Bobby again: "Do your brother a big favor, kid. Tell the cops he killed Johnny Winthrop by accident. They might even believe you."

It was impossible to tell which Wallace was speaking or if they were taking turns. The idea that they shared one demented brain struck me as a possibility. There was more struggling, but I could no longer imagine the scene.

"Here's the deal, Sammy. You're in cuffs by dark or you and little brother get the same thing Johnny got." I had no trouble imagining one of the Wallace twins slamming a heavy rock into Johnny Winthrop's skull while the other watched. And no trouble believing either twin would do the same to Sam or Bobby or anybody else who got in the way. It was time to make a move.

Carefully I began a backward body crawl, imagining myself a snake retracting from a situation that didn't allow a turn-about, however swift or silent. Back and back I eased, eyes closed tight to increase concentration. Each plant I encountered, I handled so slowly and carefully it barely let out a whisper. Instead of sticking to the path, I crawled backwards into rough, dense groundcover, not letting myself think about all the possibilities hidden in those ferns and rocks and clumps of briar-bush. I can't remember when I reached the point at which I dared to peer from my camouflage toward the direction of the scene, nor how long after that I took to my feet to make better time, dragging with me the vines and branches that wrapped my extremities. All I could do was pray I had reached a safe distance.

When I finally heard cars and people, it was all or nothing. Ripping off my restraints along with patches of skin, I put serious speed into covering ground. I had missed the trailhead but luckily stumbled into an alley not far from the hardware. The Wallace boys' truck was right where I'd seen it and, to my relief, it wasn't locked. A last burst of energy put me in the parking lot of the feed mill. I think I collapsed about the time someone yelled for my dad, "Hey, Walt! Isn't this your girl?"

* * *

You can imagine the reaction to my appearance and the baffling story I related first to my dad and then to the sheriff. You can also imagine, if you know anything about small-town Appalachia in the seventies, how Sam's outing was handled in Walker. Bobby's mother first lost her tips and then her job at Bangers. As soon as everything was wrapped up in Ohio, she and the boys would be moving to Kansas, where her sister worked on a cattle ranch. Lots of open country made it the perfect place for a fresh start. I knew I'd miss Bobby, but I couldn't wish him back to a place where no one ever lived down a sensational story.

Losing Johnny in such a scandalous way also made a profound difference for the Winthrop family, Ellen's dad resigned as mayor and her mother stayed behind pulled blinds, bound by shame and sorrow. They sent Ellen to stay with an aunt in Columbus to spare her the worst of the small-town nastiness. I decided that when Ellen returned, I'd let bygones be bygones.

The rescue boat had found Johnny's body around the same time the sheriff and his deputies discovered Bobby and Sam near the mouth of Mill Creek, pretty well beaten up, but able to tell what had happened. Johnny's appearance was somewhat altered by his time in the Muskingum. Back then, determining the cause of death was sometimes difficult, especially in river retrievals, where the bottom was rocky and the shoreline strewn with debris. And, there was the beating a body takes in the undercurrent of a dam.

Prejudicial opinion worked against the Wallace twins also. The county prosecutor and grand jury found my version of events, as well as Bobby's and Sam's, credible. Photographs of footprints made in rain-softened ground and hardened into evidence reinforced our testimony. By the end of summer, the case against the brothers was on the trial docket for autumn. No one really knows what happened to their father and Millie. I like to think a guardian angel disguised as a social worker found her a nice family to live with. That's the one part of the story that troubles me to this day.

Oh, I almost forgot to mention that in addition to the footprints, a second piece of physical evidence played a role in the decision to prosecute—a keyring, the inscription on its fob unmistakable, buried under the seat of the Wallace boys' pickup among piles of greasy tools, rotten food, and girlie magazines. It's a good thing I picked it up that day in the library. Otherwise, no one might ever have found it.

Shanksville

I.
Where the plane came down
a half-circle of hemlocks
stands dark against the sky.

II.
A call went up: one crow
in one black tree, invisible. Then
the sky was harsh with their sound.

III.
Tree became crow and crow
tree, and both the sky.

IV.
The smoky belch of the tractor
became a flock of crows, which rose
into the sky, which became
a pale-blue field.

V.
And the croaking sky became
the airplane's roar, echoing
against the grass and the grove.

VI.
The burn cooled to a char, a pyre
of dead crows, wings trembling
in the wind.

VII.
The wingprint in the earth:
a crow in full sail.

VIII.
And the smoke
lifted, and the unconscious grass
emerged.

IX.
But for the crows the field
is quiet. The forever wind,
the unbearable feet of snow.

X.
A white stone marks but
does not cover. Like bone
against the hemlocks.

XI.
Walls are built, aerodynamic,
that follow the path, the wild
lowering of the plane.

XII.
How it wobbled, unsure
if what it wanted was death
or truth.

XIII.
How the crows flew like black screams
from the sight.

XIV.
How they settled after the fire,
and the woods grew lush
again, and dark.

Language Lessons

Wordless, we entered
the forest and listened.

The language of wind,
of water, was never foreign
to us.

The languages of birds
we came to know.

Rocks spoke to us
from the beginning,
invited us into their presence.

From them we learned
how to be quiet and still.
How to stand without wavering

through darkness and cold,
when the sky falls and wind
howls all around us.

How to lift our face
in all weathers.

And how to yield
when it's time
to water's persuasion.

Taming the Creek

This morning, mist
riding the water.

The other day, pounded
by heavy rain, the creek
bucked and heaved.
It would not be broken.

Not by the clouds' stroking.
Not by the wind's soft
shushing, *therethere*.

It felt twigs and stones
roiling in its depths, under
its skin, and flailed, kicking.

No one could come close.
We had to watch
from the banks, or the backs
of bridges.

Then sun came, and sent
the rain on its way.
The creek quieted down,
found its easy pace.

Mist climbed on,
and rode it
into the morning.

Dibert's Dream: An Essay

This part of the woods stands with a quiet that seems impossible. No matter what season, what time of day, or the possibility of crowds or even stray hikers in Blue Knob State Park. Not even the routine woodland animals seem to disturb it. Perhaps this is coincidence, or just an artifact of my own imagination when I've come to visit the site. It seems appropriate, though, considering it's the spot of the discovery of the bodies of two small children in 1856.

It is a legend now, with an unfortunate surplus of truth and known facts. George and Joseph Cox wandered away from home—for some reason, never truly determined—and got lost in the woods in April of that year.

To set some historical context, in 1856, the nation was still several years away from the Civil War, although the storm clouds were gathering. Wisconsin and California had just become states a few years before, and Minnesota had not yet entered the Union. Pennsylvania, the second state to ratify the Constitution of the new United States, had been a charter member, so to speak, of the Union and would become the site of the bloodiest battle (as measured by number of casualties) in that struggle for freedom. Pennsylvania would also become the industrial powerhouse of the United States, anchored by Philadelphia and Pittsburgh, with smaller cities fueling growth and ringing the southern beltline of the state with coal mines and steel mills. Other parts of the state would be a breadbasket, with farms providing food and feed for itself and other parts of the growing nation. It would be the home of some of the world's largest companies: Carnegie Steel, Cambria Iron, the Pennsylvania Railroad.

But in 1856, the state still had huge stands of primeval forest. There was no grand Pennsylvania Railroad or Carnegie Steel, and Cambria Iron was a small operation. In this part of the state, old-growth forest rippled upward in a complex arrangement of hills, not as grand as the Rockies, but still startling in their age and complexity. This is the Allegheny Front, the eastern wall of the northern Appalachians, the formidable barrier forming the western boundary of the British Empire in the mid-18th century, almost immediately permeated by enterprising colonials. While the frontier had moved west from Pennsylvania by the mid-19th century, the forests were still there. They are, in large part, there again today, carpeting the same formidable ridge that is the Appalachians.

In 1856, the iron revolution was just beginning to stir the beginnings of the Industrial Revolution, and the people of small settlements like Pavia, in the shadows of the looming Allegheny Mountains, could easily go days or even weeks without any outside visitors. Today, Pavia Township still only has a couple hundred residents, with most of its area dominated by the three-thousand-foot tall Blue Knob Mountain, a larger than average lump in this part of the Appalachian chain. A two-lane highway winds through the contours of this wrinkled earth, and it is the only through-road in the area. It can be an exhilarating drive with a sports car –provided there aren't lugging cargo trucks or gawping tourists—and it can be also singularly terrifying in the winter no matter what one might be piloting.

There were a few trails for horses and wagons in 1856. This quiet township would have been largely silent then, and it is as if the monument built to the memories of George and Joseph Cox brought that silent past and planted it there in the forest for all to absorb.

The story, simple enough and easy to see how it might happen—so many parallels abound today—is essentially one of miscommunication and unintentional error. Some might call it parental negligence, but in April 1856, the Cox family dog barked in the woods, somewhat distant from their cabin. Believing this to be a signature of a treed gray squirrel, Samuel Cox, the father, grabbed his gun to see about the possibility of some fresh protein for the cookpot. When he left, the young boys were somewhere near the cabin; when he returned, they were gone. He had thought they had gone with his wife, Susannah, while Susannah had thought the boys had gone hunting with Samuel.

The boys, five and seven years old, were lost.

The ancient forest disclosed little; it was then and is now made of trees and secrets. Raising the alarm by the evening, all the residents in this remote and wooded area spread out and combed through the hill-sides and gullies. Within a day, there were allegedly a thousand people in the search party, a vivid picture to imagine when one realizes that carts, wagons, and horses were the only modes of transportation in a heavily forested, remote, and difficult area. Searchers lit fires at different points in the forest so that the boys might be able to find their own way to safety. Bob's Creek, still a surging stream today attracting anglers of all ages, was swollen with snowmelt; if the boys had attempted to cross it or played near it, they would have almost certainly been swept away and drowned. This is what the search parties concluded when prioritizing areas to search.

Invariably, the creeps, hucksters, and snake oilers also came to prey on the situation. Allegedly a witch took part attempting to scry for the boys, as did a dowser.

More invariably, besides the creeps, the locals put Samuel and Susannah in their crosshairs, believing that perhaps they had done away with their own sons. Why? Suspicions then would have been generated by similar phenomena to what we've seen with someone like Susan Smith in 1994, who drowned her children by driving a car into a lake. Filicide is nothing new to our era, nor to the mid-19th century.

Jacob Dibert told his wife of a dream of a child's shoe and birch trees; he also told a friend of his who recognized a description of local birch trees, which were unusual in this elevation and latitude…and which were on the other side of the swollen Bob's Creek.

On May 7, following the dream-borne clues, the bodies of the two little boys were found, huddled at the base of a tree much like what Dibert had dreamt. They had died of exposure, in a part of the woods no one had searched until after a woodsman interpreted a farmer's dream.

The tragedy then became the legend of the Lost Children of the Alleghenies.

I remember visiting the monument myself, with my father taking me there one time, more than a quarter century ago. I had known of the legend long before that but hadn't seen it in person. I've since taken visitors to the same site as a spot of historical interest; the reaction has consistently been that the experience is an almost unbearably sad one, with offerings left for the children such as toy cars, stuffed animals, cards, and handwritten notes.

The Cox parents had repairs to do for their cabin after the locals had torn up the floorboards while under the impression that the elder Coxes had done a horrific filicide; Jacob Dibert gave the Coxes the reward money that he had received for finding the children, one of several collections taken at the time and in the future, including one fifty years later which funded the construction of a monument to commemorate George and Joseph Cox. Another monument –the boys' gravestone—is in a cemetery in nearby Lovely, a small patch of homes amidst farmland and forest that warrants the name, but for the sad story in the cemetery.

The story, as many holes as it has, doesn't satisfy. It certainly doesn't satisfy most of us who would, at the very least, want to know what exactly happened to lure Joseph and George away, even those of us who know the risks in these hills and hollows. Why couldn't they get back? Why couldn't the searchers find them, and why couldn't even these small children see the fires that had been lit and found their own way back? Why had the searchers assumed that Bob's Creek was unfordable?

A lifelong hunter, I have not been lost in the woods, but, as the saying goes, I've been powerful turned around a couple of times. It's happened to me at least twice, and not far from where the Cox children were lost…just on top of that same ridge, in normal conditions and just inattentive, and then another time with my best friend while hunting and suddenly hit by a squalling, white-out of a November snowstorm. To me, it is easy to lose one's way in the Alleghenies, and I always think of these two children, dying as a warning to those of us who might not have the requisite respect for these ancient mountains. Mistakes accrue: misreading the land and the signs, not understanding the direction or the path, increasing worry, and then blind panic. The panicking lost will run in a circle; they'll hyperventilate, shedding clothes despite freezing temperatures; they'll elevate a heart rate and respiration well into blow-out territory until either that does happen, or they collapse into exhaustion and die from hypothermia.

The best thing to do is to sit down, breathe slowly and evenly, think things through, and *wait*.

That may well have been exactly what George and Joseph Cox did, and it was for naught.

The other part of the story that doesn't satisfy at least some is the idea that there must have been some type of malicious action, not even that of Samuel and Susannah Cox who, undoubtedly, were haunted by what happened to their sons until they themselves went to their own graves. Instead, the malice imagined by others stems not from human agency but some type of dark, supernatural presence. Ghost hunters might still be found lurking in the area, along with reports of children's laughter, running footsteps tormenting innocent hikers, and lingering legends of a dark witch who worked toward the evil ends of the innocent boys and sacrificed them to some malign presence.

I would offer that the true malignancy in such cases is the idea itself of the supernatural. Beyond the simple and bizarre notions of such gremlins and demons, ghosts and ghouls, there seems to be a lingering idea that the supernatural is an explanation that makes sense...when it really is not an explanation at all. Even a rudimentary explanation has some type of grounding in evidence; the supernatural has none and instead relies on imagination and fervent belief masquerading as evidence. Such true belief breeds its own brood, and it also breeds an unhealthy contempt for those that won't hew to the same supernatural subscription.

While undoubtedly skeptical, my own thoughts on the tragedy are much simpler. One does not require the supernatural to explain something that is amply explained by natural circumstances. It was, in fact, quite easy in 1856 to get lost in a huge, primeval, and isolated forest bereft of roads, cars, bikes, and truck traffic, and it was unquestionably even easier to do so as a child. So, while the ghost hunters and paranormal investigators might criticize those of us naturalists as philistines, and hold us in contempt, the far more troubling aspect of it is their contempt for the power of nature itself.

Nature is indifferent to us, and it certainly proved its indifference to the Cox children. This portion of northern Appalachia, the Allegheny Mountains, has traceable geological history going back more than three hundred million years. The Allegheny Orogeny emerged from the collision of the continents which would eventually become Africa and North America. This coincides with the Carboniferous Period, the age at which that black mineral which would fuel the Industrial Revolution in Pennsylvania, West Virginia, and elsewhere was first formed by the deposition of the first wooded and very heavily barked trees, in a time when atmospheric oxygen levels were around more than 50% higher than what they are today and the true creatures of nightmares – dragonflies with wingspans of three feet and scorpions two feet in length—freely roamed the countryside.

These ancient Alleghenies—a part of the Appalachians—have seen the rise and fall of untold species, sea levels, and land, all the way through the short, sad lives of the Cox children and continuing through today, where the remnants of those heavily barked, three-hundred-million-year-old trees are still being mined for fuel and energy. The times from giant insects through Jacob Dibert's dream have all stood witness to tragedy and triumph, always the eternal cycle. There is no need for a ghost, a witch, a demon, or the laughter of haunting children.

Still, one can visit the monument to the Lost Children of Alleghenies and listen to that silence, be it summer or be it winter. It is the silent weight of hundreds of millions of years of history, of deep time, and the knowledge that these hills will continue to be here for hundreds of millions of years past the time when we all have gone the way of George and Joseph Cox. It doesn't require the prestidigitation of video editing of ghostly orbs; it requires only humility and understanding that what we see and learn is the history of nature, and the nature of history. What we all have, instead, is this moment to watch the sunrise and sunset over these hills, and pause, and remember to imagine what these hills have witnessed, with or without us.

That Which Doesn't Kill Us

When I was in grade school, I was told the Nile flowed north and the Monongahela flowed north and that was rare for rivers and weren't we special to have a north-flowing river in Pittsburgh.

We were also told that we lived just outside the 6-mile radius that would allow us to survive a nuclear bomb. Pittsburgh was super important in manufacturing so much steel, and weren't we special that we were so productive we would be an attractive target, but don't worry, we would survive. We weren't told we might be very severely burned or blinded by the flash, or in any way maimed, so I felt reassured.

With the bomb business out of the way, I got back to thinking that I would like to be like Mark Twain and float down my hometown rivers that merged into the Mississippi, rivers so special that two formed the beginning of one, the Ohio. The confluence of all three excited entrepreneurs into building the industry that would possibly kill me by attracting enemy fire. The roaring steel industry. When my fifth-grade self wanted to Huckleberry Finn it down the river, death threatened from the very rivers I loved, from a different source than I'd been taught to fear.

It's no secret that Pittsburgh had a legendary pollution problem. My father told stories of the lampposts that would loom out of the dark gray daylight and guide him as he walked to school. He touched each one as he walked by. My first-grade teacher would recount us, when we settled back into our wooden desks after our bathroom break, that when she was younger, on the days she wore a sleeveless dress, she would have to wash all the way up to her shoulders after she washed her hands, otherwise there would be a line around her wrist. We looked at our own arms and wrists. It was her way of reminding us to wash our hands. I never forgot the line of soot.

A photo taken at the corner of Fifth and Liberty Avenues in 1940 encapsulates the time. The street looks slick, as if just after a rain, the lights of store fronts and signs brightly reflect the pavement and car head-lights, brilliant as the dazzle of Times Square at 10:55 PM. The time of the photo is 10:55 AM.

Twenty-five years after this photo, in the mid 1960s, the sky looked blue, although the mills were still dumping into the river with regularity and the skies at night still glowed. As a child, I'd watch the nightly glow in the southern sky from my front door, the north-flowing Monongahela to the south of our neighborhood. The mills that lit up the night felt satisfying because it meant people were working and our city was success-ful, and that made my young eyes feel secure.

* * *

I didn't swim in the rivers. I didn't think anyone did, but I did think of them as the beautiful lifeblood of the city, even as the pollution was moving through them. In 2019, after a long absence from Pittsburgh, I'd find opportunities to catch the glint of sun off the Monongahela. Boats tied up in basins looking ready for a day of floating tugged at my longing to be on the water. My lunchtime daydream gaze of the Ohio is interrupted when a work friend suddenly interjects, "I hate the river."

He is older than I am by nearly twenty years. He played in the rivers as a child. He remembers the industrial foam, like airy milk, coming up as high as his knees as he waded into the water.

"But I would still do it," he says, shrugging in response to my raised eyebrow. "We would dive off a bridge when I was a few years older. Well. I didn't, but the older boys did. I watched them. And one night, two of my friends died."

He is quiet.

"How?" I ask.

"The current," he said, "swept them under a barge. They surfaced under the barge and couldn't get to air in time. Found the bodies a couple days later." He nods in the direction of the sparkling river behind me. "The river is ugly to me." Another pause. "I still remember animal guts from the slaughterhouses dumped into the river." He looks at me almost apologetically, "You're eating. I shouldn't tell you that."

Those rivers, dirty and clean, hold so many stories that I've only glimpsed. The stories my mother's father told me with a chuckle of his stealing watermelons off the barges as a hungry young man. My uncle's father stacked watermelons on the barges, his first job as a recent immigrant. The only job he was qualified to do. No English required.

The Ohio, the largest tributary by volume to the Mississippi, the "Westward, Ho" river that for a while made Pittsburgh the "Gateway to the West," is still the most polluted waterway in the country. The Clean Water Act helped reduce the discharge of pollutants into the water, but the Ohio is yet again under siege. Chemical plants are poised to dump plastics and petrochemicals. Pollution controls are poised for a roll back, and residents along the river may long deal with the repercussions of industrial waste, even if industries ultimately choose to move away.

In a book, I see old pictures of the long-standing slag heap located off the Parkway East, the refuse from industrial dumping. I'm reminded of the familiar mass that I saw nearly daily before leaving Pittsburgh for college. Now, an expensive housing development flourishes on top of the old slag. When I first saw the newly built neighborhood, Summerset, I laughed. "You're buying a house on top of a slag heap?" But, yes, I thought, it was a clever way to recycle land. Still, I also wondered if there were residual chemicals under the fresh groomed lawns. The residents of the previous neighborhood fought the invasion of the growing slag mountain that threatened their houses and health. The ravine they called home no longer exists, only the slag top development they could never afford.

* * *

Only recently did I discover that there once was a bridge between Carnegie Library and Forbes Field, crossing in front of where the towering Cathedral of Learning would one day be built. Balconies set along the bridge allowed pedestrians to pause and look out at the natural world of the ravine far below. Then Saint Pierre's Ravine was filled in. Saint Pierre's Ravine in Oakland reminded me of the loss of Glen Canyon, Colorado; both were beautiful wonders and ecosystems lost to progress. Early on, what was once Saint Pierre's Ravine became a parking lot. Today it is a park of sorts and filled with coffee stands and a small carousel. A touch of greenery reclaimed and restored.

A large ravine remains between Carnegie Library, Phipps's Conservatory, and Carnegie Mellon University. From the bridge between there is a good view of the "Cloud Factory" column Michael Chabon talks about in *Mysteries of Pittsburgh*. Puffs of smoke against a flat dark night emerge like perfect clouds. What lies below is Junction Hollow, a ravine so deep and large, train tracks run through, and a community dots the bottom.

* * *

When I think of Saint Pierre's, I wonder what other parts of Pittsburgh's natural world were filled in, lost to changing times. Two million years of erosion of the Allegheny Plateau, advanced by effects of the Pleistocene Ice Age one million years ago, changed the course of water that flowed through the region which would one day be Pittsburgh. Before the Ice Age, Pittsburgh had one river. Geologists called it the Pittsburgh River and its flow completely isolated areas. For example, the region that would become Squirrel Hill, profoundly isolated by geological formation, was so inaccessible it would take the advent of the trolley to entice occupants. Ice sheets several thousand feet thick dammed the pre-Ice Age river. Backed-up water formed a drainage zone. The water then breached topographic divides and eroded enough land to give flow to the newly formed Ohio, Allegheny, and Monongahela rivers. Deep hollows and ravines remained as the water receded into new paths.

Ironically, the loss of Glen Canyon proved the saving of the Grand Canyon. Developers had already been looking to the future damming of the Grand Canyon when the uproar of Glen Canyon's demise halted the plans. The rust-belting of the steel industry opened potential for saving riverside land.

* * *

I never hitchhiked down the Ohio, of course, but standing near the fountain at the Point and staring down the flowing expanse ignited my dreams of river adventures. And I took them. I lived with gentle flow of the upper Colorado river a constant in my daily view and working life, and it still resonates like a distant echo. Yet, as I stood at the very beginning of the Ohio River with visions of Mark Twain heading to the Mississippi Delta, the beautiful view diverted my attention from what was lurking below the surface.

We celebrate Pittsburgh's rivers as being special, so by extension *we* are special. The city is represented with beautiful photographs of the golden triangle, the sight breathtaking on first view emerging from the Fort Pitt tunnels. To this day, I look forward to that initial glimpse of the point of the Ohio. Bike paths line the rivers and pleasure boats proliferate, but our drinking water is threatened, and the poison is invisible. We are not caring for our waterways in more than cosmetic terms. Our skies will never again be night at noon from roaring steel mills, but there is a current plastic bomb that threatens from different manufacturing. It spreads like nuclear fallout that knows no mileage limit. It would not protect the little girl ducking under a desk for yet another training drill. Its reach extends as far as anyone who drinks a glass of water.

What Is Worse

Following the splashes of blood wandering over the world
—Galway Kinnell, "The Bear"

What if there is no blood?
In the air, no hum of bees or dragonflies?
No slink of minnows in the chromium stream?
What if soon there is no earned and painful death,
just "a patient etherized upon a table,"
being now the earth,
and weather becomes punishment—
rain, fire, wind the names of enemies
of our own invention?

Still the small thunder of jets high up,
bombs gorging their billion-dollar innards,
still the stink-hiss of traffic on the stalled rivers of asphalt,
still the diesel hymns of freight trains hauling parts of the world
to other parts of the world in the grand displacement,
the breaking mix, the moil.

How long I have been a part of it.
How long my comfort has cost the world.
Almost everything is, at last, smoke of my fires,
ash of my habits, fumes
of my heartless demands,
swirling over the embers of the world
from my greed's dark thurible.

And what if my hands still seem clean, nothing to wash guiltily off:
no sign warning *The End is Near* at the end of the road
I have bum-rushed my life along?

At the End of the Day

—the phrase drained of meaning, dredged
like the Altoona lake where carp and bass and bluegills
flap in sediment below the dam.

   [Some of the fish old enough to vote.]

At the end of the day, Mars is the brightest it's been
in a decade. After sunset, look east for the rusty tinge.

   [Its surface rich in iron oxide.]

At the end of the day, a call from the grown daughter
still on your cell phone plan, her cheek pressed against glass
fitted by a worker who solders three screens a minute,
twelve hours a shift.

   [*Solders*, so close to *soldiers*.]

At the end of the day, a once-feral cat falls asleep
in your lap, its prehensile paw gripping your hand.

   [Is *hensile* a word?]

At the end of the day, the cornfield is still
flattened by the minivan that careened
off the road in a head-on crash.

   [Tinny sirens in the distance, blood
   on the steering wheel, blood in the mouth.]

At the end of the day, children are sleeping
on concrete, covered only by Mylar blankets
the color of shiny dimes.

   [Think March of Dimes, dime bag.]

At the end of the day, darkness is a room
we double-lock with a rusty key.

[I've used *rusty* twice. I really don't care, do you?]

At the end of the day we can't let ourselves dwell
on the fish or the children.

[*Sediment*, so close to *sentiment*.]

At the end of the day, I dream our kitchen counters
are too high. We raise the floors, plank by grainy
wooden plank, like lake water after a storm.

[At the end of the day, we have a granite island,
a Cuisinart toaster oven, an electric tea kettle.]

The fish can't be relocated, something about invasive species.
The parents can't be located, something about
cruel bureaucracies.

[At the end of the day, he knew,
they knew, we knew.]

At the end of the day, blood tastes like metal.

[Does metal taste like blood?]

At the end of the day, I retreat to the luxury
of pin-fitted syllables on a page.

[*Page*, so close to *cage*.]

At the end of the day, we all seek our own level.

State of Connecticut

Is what I've breathed for twenty-seven years.
Is where I created two lives,
coddled my pets, sold my Appalachian heritage

down the river of neglect. It's a state
of blue sky, ochre rock, woodland birds
flying straight in from childhood dreams.

It's the land of *ahnts,* not *ants,*
nyther, eyether, and not ending thoughts
with a preposition. Here winter begins

on the appointed day, not a Pittsburgh
November, and spring may not arrive
until a cruel April sends regrets.

The rocky coastline is there to see
only if you own it, the majestic Merritt
full of blind contestants. But where are

the stout evergreens landlocked
and buried in snow? The sultry summers
and scallions set out in March?

The wide brick porches of Federalist homes,
their painted floors covered in faux carpet?
Plastic nativity scenes in December,

beds of red geranium and pink petunia?
The Allegheny foothills folded around
ghost steel mills, and the passing shadows

of magnificent lives extinguished,
their beautiful tales of love and separation
gone up to meet a hazy sky?

Our Homeless River

Evicted from its bed
beneath the sycamores
and shoved into the open
where it cuts

through grassland
and rushes east to join
a family of rivers
headed to the Gulf,

into the mouth
of roaring hurricanes
and the warm salt sea.
It wriggles and twists,

jumps its banks,
runs mud-colored
and swift, swallows
souls. Our river

is uneasy in its bed,
it tosses and turns,
sends its nightmares
into our sleep.

We wake
startled, with salt
on our cheeks, wondering
why we cry.

CONTRIBUTOR BIOS

Rachel Allen

Rachel Allen is an emerging writer in Johnstown, Pa. She works as a Certified Music Practitioner playing the harp in hospice, and she teaches trauma-informed yoga in community settings. Allen is part of the blog team at Christians Practicing Yoga; she has a byline in the *Tribune Democrat* and has published pieces in *Hags on Fire* and Long Shot Books Publishing House. She lives with her husband and Japanese Chin dog and has two adult children.

Kathy B. Austin

Kathy B. Austin has published in Writing Path 1 anthology (University of Iowa Press), *Buddhist Poetry Journal, Poppy Road Review*, and *Mock Turtle Zine*, among others. Awards include the Dayton Metro Library, Iowa Poetry Day, and Paul Laurence Dunbar competitions. Her poems have been aired on Conrad's Corner, WYSO 91.3.

Joel Burcat

Joel Burcat has published short stories and two environmental legal thrillers: *Drink to Every Beast* (2019) and *Amid Range* (2021). His novel, *Strange Fire*, about fracking, is due out in 2022. He was the 2019 Lawyer of the Year in Environmental Litigation (for Central Pennsylvania, Best Lawyers in America).

Anthony Clemons

Anthony Clemons is an Appalachian writer. His work has appeared in *Harvard Review, Hippocampus Magazine, The Daily Drunk*, and elsewhere. He holds an MFA in Nonfiction Writing from Goucher College. You can read his work and other musings at anthonycclemons.com and follow him on Twitter and Instagram @anthonycclemons.

Jessica Cory

Jessica Cory hails from Chillicothe, Ohio and now lives in western North Carolina, teaching English at Western Carolina University. She is the editor of Mountains Piled upon Mountains: *Appalachian Nature Writing in the Anthropocene* (WVU Press, 2019), and her work has appeared in many regional and national publications.

Mary Alice Dixon

Mary Alice Dixon is a Pittsburgh native, former professor, and Yale MA. Her work appears in numerous publications, including *Main Street Rag*, *Fourth River*, *Broad River Review*, *Kakalak*, *moonShine Review*, *North Dakota Quarterly*, *Pinesong*, and *Stonecoast Review*. She lives in North Carolina's red clay but carries coal in her bones.

Ken Gournic

Gournic spent his last dozen years in the Pittsburgh Division of the United States Postal Inspection Service. He worked several fraud cases in the Northern District of West Virginia at the U. S. Attorney's offices in Wheeling, Clarksburg, and Martinsburg. The people and places he came in contact with made up some of the best experiences of his professional life. Gournic retired from that position after 36 years, then enrolled in the Writing Certificate Program at the University of Pittsburgh. That experience was so enjoyable for him; the doing of it, regardless of success or failure, was worth every single moment spent.

Richard Hague

Richard Hague is a native of Steubenville, Ohio and author or editor of 20 volumes, including *Riparian: Poetry, Short Prose, and Photographs Inspired by the Ohio River*, edited with Sherry Cook Stanforth (Dos Madres Press, 2019). He continues as an Artist-in-Residence at Thomas More University in northern Kentucky.

Lisa Harris

Lisa Harris writes poetry, novels and personal essays. Her novels are 'Geechee Girls, Allegheny Dream, and The Raven's Tale (Ravenna Press). Her poetry books include *Traveling Through Glass, Dwelling Place*, (from Cayuga Lake Books), and *Broken Open*, (Wasteland Press). She is from Snow Shoe, PA.

Jennifer Jenkins

Jennifer Jenkins' novel, American Bourbon, was released in June 2021. She has written for *NonBinary Review*, *Hippocampus Magazine*, *Up North Lit*, *Canopy Review*, and *Parentheses Journal*. She was nominated for a PEN America Short Story Award and earned two honorable mentions for the fiction award from *Glimmer Train*.

Cathy Cultice Lentes

Cathy Cultice Lentes lives and writes in southeast Ohio. She holds an MFA from the Solstice Program of Pine Manor College and is the author of *Getting the Mail* (Finishing Line Press, 2016). Her work appears in various literary journals, and anthologies, as well as publications for children.

Wendy McVicker

Wendy McVicker is current Poet Laureate of Athens, Ohio, where she has lived by the river and among the green hills since 1985. Her most recent collection is the chapbook, *Zero, a Door*, published by The Orchard Street Press in 2021.

Jean Mikhail

Jean Mikhail has lived in Athens, Ohio most of her life, and is proud to call it home. She has published in *Fifth Wednesday Journal*, *Riverwind*, and an anthology called #Queer, as well as other journals. She also belongs to an old-time fiddle band called "The Trophy Wives."

Ben Moyer

Ben Moyer's writing about nature and outdoors appears in numerous regional and national publications. He is a past winner of the Outdoor Writers Association of America's Excellence in Craft Award, honoring lifetime body of work. *On Work and Being Paid* is his first foray into writing about work and family within small business in Northern Appalachia.

Erin Murphy

Erin Murphy is Professor of English at Penn State Altoona. Her latest book, *Human Resources*, is forthcoming from Salmon Poetry. Her work has appeared/is forthcoming in *Diode*, *Southern Poetry Review*, *Women's Studies Quarterly*, and elsewhere. Her awards include the Dorothy Sargent Rosenberg Poetry Prize and Best of the Net award.

Karen Whittingon Nelson

Karen Whittington Nelson writes poetry and fiction from her home on a small southeastern Ohio farm. Her work has been published in *Northern Appalachia Review, Volume 2*, the *Anthology of Appalachian Writers, Volumes 12 and 13*, the *WOAP/Women Speak Anthologies, Volumes 2-6*, and the forthcoming *Vol 7, Gyroscope Review and Pudding Magazine*.

Ryan Richard Nych

Ryan Richard Nych is a resident of Western Pennsylvania, a husband and father, an educator, an avid outdoorsman, a hobby farmer, and a member of Pennsylvania Outdoor Writers Association (POWA).

Joshua Penrod

Joshua Penrod is a native of the area and has personally visited the shrine described in his essay, along with the woods in which it is located. He has a Ph.D. in Science and Technology Studies from Virginia Tech, and has recently published *Johnstown Industry* with Arcadia Publishing, a photo-heavy work comparing the industrial history with the post-industrial present.

Bonnie Proudfoot

Bonnie Proudfoot has published fiction and poetry in journals, including *Northern Appalachia Review, Kestrel, Sheila-Na-Gig, Pine Mountain Sand and Gravel*. Her novel, *Goshen Road*, (Swallow Press, 2020) was selected by the Women's National Book Association for its Great Group Reads. It was also long-listed for the 2021 PEN/ Hemingway award.

Mark Saba

Saba's publications include, most recently, Two Novellas: *A Luke of All Ages/Fire and Ice* (fiction), *Calling the Names* (poetry) and *Ghost Tracks: Stories of Pittsburgh Past*. He is also a painter, and he is recently retired as a medical illustrator at Yale University. Please see marksabawriter.com.

JL Silverman

JL Silverman is an MFA Creative Non-Fiction 2020 graduate of Chatham University, with a concentration in nature writing. JL's work has been published with *Ekphrastic Review, Huffington Post, The Under Review, Celestal Review*, Chatham's school newspaper *The Communique*, the *Griffith Observer*, and the medical journals *Imaging Economics and CLP*.

Lois Spencer

Lois Spencer's publishing credits include *Ohio Teachers Write, Iris, Anthology of Appalachian Writers, The Poorhouse Rag*, and *Women Speak*. She earned two Ohio University degrees, BSED and MSED and her MALL at Marietta College. A memoir, *In the Language of My Country* (Outskirts Press 2017), highlights a uniquely Appalachian experience.

Beverly Voigt

Beverly Voigt, a native of Pittsburgh, is a winner of the Friends of Acadia Poetry Prize and a Pushcart Prize nominee. Her chapbook, *Woman of Salt*, was published by Seven Kitchens Press (2018). A new chapbook, *Song of the Overcast*, will be released by Finishing Line Press in February 2022.

Randi Ward

Randi Ward is a poet, translator, lyricist, and photographer from Belleville, WV. She earned her MA in Cultural Studies from the University of the Faroe Islands and is a recipient of the American-Scandinavian Foundation's Nadia Christensen Prize. Her work has been featured on Folk Radio UK, NPR, and PBS NewsHour. www.randiward.com

Jerry Wemple

Jerry Wemple is the author of three full-length poetry collections, most recently *Artemas & Ark: the Ridge and Valley Poems*, and two poetry chapbooks. His nonfiction work has been published in Ninth Letter, Ozy.com, and other venues. He teaches in the creative writing program at Bloomsburg University of Pennsylvania.